MOVE ANYWAY

A GUIDE FOR OVERTHINKERS, PERFECTIONISTS, AND ALMOST-STARTERS

Book Design by Kelsey Ann Darilus and Alec Giorgio

To Him, for giving me the ultimate push
(a shove, really)…it's made all the difference.

CONTENTS

INTRODUCTION

You're Not Lazy, You're Stuck!

You've got notebooks full of ideas, a camera roll of screenshots for "later," and a voice inside you that knows you're capable of more. And yet, you hesitate. You plan. You wait. You scroll through what everyone else seems to be doing, wondering if your moment already passed. You wait for a better time, a sign, the right mood, the clarity to strike. But it doesn't. So you shrink. You second-guess. And the dream that once made your heart beat faster gets pushed further and further back on the shelf. Sound familiar?

If you're reading this, I imagine you're not short on ambition, talent, or ideas. Chances are you've already thought about what you want (maybe even more than once). You've envisioned something new for your life. Perhaps it's launching a creative project, changing careers, setting stronger boundaries, moving cities, starting therapy, or finally finishing that thing you've been discussing for far too long. You've talked about it, maybe even journaled about it, taken courses, brainstormed with a coach, listened to podcasts, tried to psych yourself up...

And yet, you still feel stuck. For all your knowledge, you feel stuck in place.

Let me go ahead and say this now: you are not broken. You are not lazy. You are not crazy for feeling a little lost when your head is full of wisdom and your calendar is full of commitments. You're simply caught in that frustrating, foggy space between knowing and moving.

And I get it because I've been there too.

I know what it feels like to sit at the crossroads of clarity and chaos, deciding if what you feel inside is worth disrupting everything around you. I know the weight of staring at a path that no longer fits and still asking yourself, "But what will they think if I leave it?"

I've left big, respectable jobs with fancy titles when I knew they were no longer aligned with the life I was called to live. I've ended relationships and friendships that once felt essential, until I realized I was shrinking myself to stay in them. I've moved cities, including a major decision to relocate from North Carolina to Dallas, Texas, not because it was part of a grand plan, but because something inside me whispered, "It's time to start fresh."

Allow me to be transparent. None of those decisions came easy. I didn't have it all figured out. There were moments I cried behind closed doors, wrestled with guilt and self-doubt, and wondered if I was ruining something that everyone else admired. I longed for a blueprint, something to confirm I was making the right call. And as a woman of faith, I carried the extra weight of not wanting to disappoint God. I didn't want to move ahead of His timing or assume I knew better than the plan He destined for my life. That tension – between obedience and uncertainty – was real, and it forced me to get still, listen closely, and trust that God wasn't just present in the clarity, but He was also holding me up while I wrestled with the confusion.

The "blueprints" I found felt stale, outdated, and unfit for the kind of life I was trying to build. They didn't account for nuance. For imagination. For faith. For the gut-deep knowing that this version of your life doesn't reflect your power, purpose, or potential.

So, I started creating my own. I leaned into my BOLDprint (more on that later in the book).

This book is one small part of that journey, but a meaningful one. It's my way of handing you a flashlight as you stand at your own fork in the road – whether it's personal, professional, emotional, or spiritual. I'm not here to give you all the answers. I'm here to help you move forward with a little more clarity, hope, courage, and boldness.

You've Got Company on This Journey

As we journey through this guide together, you'll meet three characters – fictional, but deeply rooted in real experiences and patterns I've seen in myself, my clients, and the countless brilliant people I've had the privilege to know and walk alongside. Their stories might sound like yours – you're not alone, but meet the others who have been stuck too.

Overton is our overthinker. He's analytical, smart, thoughtful – maybe too thoughtful. He can see all sides of every decision, sometimes making choosing feel impossible. He's often praised for how thoroughly he prepares, but beneath that preparation is a fear of getting it wrong, of missing something important, of not being enough.

Patti is the perfectionist. She's the checklist queen, the one who excels in everything she touches... until it's time to do something new, unfamiliar, or deeply personal. Patti holds herself to impossible standards and worries that she shouldn't do it at all if she can't do it perfectly. So, she stays busy, productive, but not fulfilled.

Alex is the almost-starter. Their heart is full of ideas, their head is full of dreams, but something always seems to get in the way. They get close, so close, to starting, but back away at the last moment. Not because they don't care, but because the fear of failing, or even the fear of success, feels too heavy to carry alone. Besides, they're more comfortable following the path of someone else who is willing to lead the way instead, even when they know there's a better way to go.

You might find yourself in just one of them. And it's okay if a mix of all three stories collectively feels familiar to your journey. Wherever you land, I want you to know this: feeling stuck doesn't make you weak, it makes you human. And your desire for something more? That's not a burden. It's a clue.

What to Expect (and What Not To)

This isn't another self-help book filled with motivational quotes and unrealistic promises. It's not about hustling harder, nor is it about faking confidence until you finally believe it.

What you'll find here is a blend of real talk, practical tools, and guided reflection. We'll unpack how perfectionism masks fear, and why comparison hijacks your progress. We'll also explore how your brain processes fear and uncertainty, why you default to planning or procrastination, and how tiny, repeatable actions – what I call micro-boldness – can disrupt your patterns and get you moving again. In addition to sharing lessons learned from my personal story, I'll also share examples from Overton, Patti, and Alex's stories about how they broke through stagnation caused by overthinking, perfectionism, and false starts. Their stories are not about massive overhauls, but tiny, consistent acts of courage – even when the full path wasn't visible.

Also, here's something important to know about me: I'm a Christian! So, alongside the science, strategy, and storytelling, you'll also see glimpses of my faith woven throughout this book. I'll reference scripture, spiritual wisdom, and how my belief in God has shaped my understanding of courage, calling, and purpose. If that's new for you, or not your belief system, that's okay, take what serves you. My goal is never to force my faith onto others, but to offer the full truth of how I've learned to move anyway.

And most importantly, this is a workbook. A living guide. You'll find trackers, tools, and exercises throughout to help you move – not just in your thoughts but your life. I encourage you to write in the margins, fill out the journal prompts directly inside of the book, or feel free to use a separate journal or notepad to jot down your thoughts in a separate place. Just do the work!

This isn't a textbook or a cheerleading manual. It's a guide for people who know they're meant for more but aren't sure how to get moving. It's for people who've almost started five different things but finished none. For people who carry incredible ideas in their heads but feel overwhelmed when it's time to bring them to life. For those who silently wrestle with the pressure to get it right the first time.

Each chapter is designed to help you confront what's been holding you back and walk away with something more valuable than confidence: a strategy. You don't have to be fearless to start. You don't even have to know exactly where you're going. You just have to be willing to go. You have to decide that where you are right now isn't where you want to stay. It's time to break the hold that fear, perfectionism, comparison, and uncertainty have had on your momentum.

So if you're an overthinker, a perfectionist, or someone who's brilliant at planning but scared of the messiness of action, you're in the right place. This isn't about becoming a new person. It's about reconnecting with the powerful one you already are. Boldness isn't just a personality trait; it's a neurological skill. You can strengthen and retrain one, even if it feels shaky at first. One that builds with every small, intentional use.

So, take a deep breath. Unclench your grip on needing it all to be clear. And get ready to move – messily, bravely, and boldly. You don't have to know the entire path. You just need to take the first two steps. Let's shake off the shame of being stuck and replace it with a strategy for moving forward, one imperfect step at a time.

When I finally gave myself permission to stop overthinking and start doing, even before I felt "qualified", everything changed. Not overnight, and not without setbacks. But it changed. Because movement generates clarity. Action builds confidence. And momentum? That's the game-changer. You don't need a magic wand or a fully developed plan. You need a next move (or two), and I'm here to help you find it.

Let's move anyway!

Chapter 1

STUCK IS A SIGNAL, NOT A SENTENCE

I don't have to wait for fear to leave. I only have to prove to myself that it can't hold me back.

Have you ever felt like you're pressing the gas on your dreams while your foot is still on the brake? You're not imagining things. That push-pull tension – the desire to move paired with the instinct to retreat – isn't a flaw. It's a signal. And it comes from one of the most powerful systems in your body: your brain.

In this chapter, we're not just talking about motivation. We're going deeper into the patterns, protection mechanisms, and wiring that shape how we respond to risk, boldness, and uncertainty. Because once you understand the science behind why you feel stuck, you'll also begin to understand how to move.

You've likely tried to shake it off. Told yourself to "just start" or "get over it." Maybe you've even convinced yourself that other people just have something you don't, like more courage, clarity, and confidence. But what if the problem isn't your motivation or mindset? What if the real story is happening behind the scenes in your biology, wiring, and the patterns your brain has been trained to protect?

This chapter isn't here to hype you up with surface-level motivation. It's here to help you understand why you feel stuck in the first place, and what to do about it. Because when you understand what your brain is trying to do, you can respond with strategy instead of shame. You can learn to recognize the resistance not as a stop sign, but as a doorway. One that invites you to retrain your brain and reclaim your momentum.

So if boldness hasn't come easy for you, it's not because you're missing something; it's because your brain has been doing what it was designed to do: keep you safe. But safety and growth don't always walk hand in hand. To move forward, we have to understand what's happening inside our minds when fear shows up, and how we can begin to rewire it.

Your Brain Remembers Fear, But It Can Learn Courage

Before we can shift how we respond to fear, we have to understand what's actually happening underneath it. The resistance you feel isn't random; it results from patterns your brain has carefully constructed over time, designed to keep you from getting hurt again. Most people think boldness is something you're either born with or you're not. That some people are just naturally fearless – skydiving, start-up-launching, public-speaking unicorns – while the rest of us sit on the sidelines, watching from behind our laptops with a heart full of hesitation and a browser full of unopened tabs labeled "someday." But here's the truth: boldness isn't a personality trait reserved for the extroverted or the ultra-confident. It's actually something far more universal, and far more trainable. Boldness is a neurological skill. And just like any other skill, it can be learned, practiced, and strengthened over time.

A group of researchers led by Andreas Frick published a study, *Dopamine and fear memory formation in the human amygdala*[1], that explored how dopamine, commonly known as the brain's "feel-good" chemical, interacts with the amygdala, the region of the brain that

1. Frick A, Björkstrand J, Lubberink M, Eriksson A, Fredrikson M, Åhs F. Dopamine and fear memory formation in the human amygdala. Mol Psychiatry. 2022 Mar;27(3):1704-1711. doi: 10.1038/s41380-021-01400-x. Epub 2021 Dec 3. PMID: 34862441; PMCID: PMC9095491

processes fear. What they found was fascinating: dopamine doesn't just motivate us or make us feel rewarded. It also plays a powerful role in helping our brain encode and store fear-based memories.[1] This means that even when you're not in actual physical danger, your brain can still respond to emotionally vulnerable situations – like pressing send on that email, sharing your creative idea, or putting yourself out there – as if your safety were at risk. In other words, the same system that helps us avoid real threats can also convince us to abandon big dreams.

So when you freeze, stall, or suddenly decide that now is the perfect time to re-alphabetize your spice rack instead of finishing that business proposal, it's not because you're flaky or unmotivated. It's because your brain is doing what it was wired to do: keep you safe from anything that feels unfamiliar, uncertain, or potentially painful.

Here's the part that changes everything: if the brain can learn fear, it can also learn courage. Every time you take a micro-bold action, something I define as a step (or two) that feels intentional, meaningful, and even a little scary, you begin to create new neurological pathways. Over time, those steps signal to your brain, "This risk didn't destroy me. In fact, I'm still standing." And that repetition begins to build a new kind of safety, one rooted not in retreating from fear, but in moving forward with it.

So no, you're not broken. You're not just "not brave." You're human. And you're working with a brain that remembers what hurt; but is also ready to learn what helps. That learning begins with small steps. Boldness doesn't have to show up loud or flashy – the way that traditional boldness has been defined. It can be quiet. Subtle. Uneven. It can look like saying "yes" to something before you feel fully ready or choosing to share your idea even when your voice shakes.

Take the example of someone who speaks up in a meeting for the first time after years of staying silent. Their heart races, palms sweat, and the inner critic is screaming. But they do it anyway. The world doesn't end. In fact, someone nods in agreement. That moment gets stored, not as fear, but as survival. As success. The next time it's a little easier. That's not luck. That's neurological retraining. Or maybe it's a new entrepreneur who finally hits "publish" on their first offer after weeks of second-guessing. One click. One choice. But it reclaims an entire narrative that once said, don't be too visible, don't take up too much space.

These moments don't erase fear, but they rewrite what it means. They teach your brain that courage doesn't require the absence of risk, only the willingness to walk through it.

And that's exactly what I had to learn in one of the most uncertain, high-pressure seasons of my own leadership journey. Let me take you back to the very beginning of that chapter.

Afraid, But Leading Anyway

When people hear the title of Chief Operating Officer, or "COO," they often imagine someone confident, composed, and sure of their every move. But what most don't see is the quiet wrestling that happens behind the scenes, the doubts that creep in, especially when you're walking into something new, something big, and something that asks more of you than you've ever been asked before.

I'll never forget the moment I was named COO of a healthcare startup. On paper, it looked like the perfect role that blended my love for strategy, leadership, and operational design. It was the kind of job people aspire to. But beneath the surface, I was flooded with doubt. I was stepping into a room filled with seasoned executives who had already held C-suite titles for a few years, most of whom were older than me, and many had been in leadership longer than I'd been in the industry. And now, I was expected to cast a vision, build the operational infrastructure, and guide the entire team forward.

I wanted to rise to the occasion, but part of me still wrestled with imposter syndrome. What if I wasn't enough? What if they saw through me? What if I got it wrong, made a costly mistake, or proved the inner critic right? I didn't have all the answers. I didn't have a blueprint. But I did have a choice, to either let fear paralyze me or find a way to move anyway.

So, I started small. I began by creating a new rhythm in our weekly staff meetings. I introduced something called a "belonging moment" which allowed us to get to know one another beyond our roles at work. One way to connect during a belonging moment was to encourage each team member, me included, to name one small, bold, yet intentional action they would commit to for the week ahead. It didn't have to be groundbreaking. It just had to be meaningful. Some people committed to having difficult conversations they'd been avoiding. Others raised ideas they'd been sitting on for months. Some set boundaries for the first time in their careers.

At first, the energy in the room was cautious. People weren't sure what "bold" really meant. They weren't used to naming their fears aloud, let alone being encouraged to take risks. But slowly, something started to shift. The act of naming their micro-bold move out loud gave people a reason to act, and the support to follow through. Our staff meetings transformed from routine check-ins to moments of activation and accountability. People weren't just planning tasks – they were practicing courage.

And what moved me most was watching how those tiny declarations helped people get unstuck, not in grand, sweeping ways, but in deeply human, practical ones. They started to trust their own voices. They stopped waiting for permission. And even when fear showed up, they began to move anyway.

I didn't become fearless overnight. But I learned how to become skilled in operating in boldness. I became skilled in what it means to act in the face of uncertainty, and to build a team culture where movement matters more than perfection. That's what micro-boldness gave my team and me. It didn't erase the pressure we felt; it gave us a way to move through it, one small act at a time.

My experience in that leadership role taught me something I haven't forgotten; it's not just executives or high performers who struggle with movement. The fear of getting it wrong, the habit of hesitating, the loop of avoidance, all of that lives in everyday moments, no matter what season of life you're in. I've seen it in colleagues, clients, and community members. I've seen it in students and seasoned professionals. I've seen it in the stories of people just like you. Let's bring back Overton, Patti, and Alex. Their patterns may differ, but at the core, they're all navigating the same thing: a brain that learned how to protect them – and now has to learn how to let them move.

Different Patterns, Same Pause

When Thinking Too Much Becomes a Safety Net

Overton is the kind of person people turn to when they need thoughtful advice. He's measured, analytical, and rarely makes a decision without weighing every angle. He takes pride in being thorough, and that habit has served him well for most of his life. But lately, Overton has been quietly carrying something heavy: an idea he can't seem to act on.

He's been dreaming about launching a consulting business for the past two years. He's done everything that makes it look like progress; he's read the books, taken the webinars, drafted business names, and built and scrapped three versions of a website. On the surface, it seems like he's preparing. But under the surface, he's stuck.

What Overton doesn't realize yet is that his pattern of overthinking is a form of self-protection. His brain has associated forward movement with risk – the risk of being judged, failing publicly and not living up to his own high expectations. So instead of taking action, his nervous system redirects him back to what feels safer: research, revision, rework.

It's not that Overton lacks motivation. It's that his brain, in an effort to keep him emotionally safe, has built a habit loop around caution. That loop is familiar; the more familiar it becomes, the harder it is to disrupt.

Overton's shift began when he stopped waiting to feel "certain" and asked himself what small, bold step he could take, even with the present uncertainty. His first micro-bold move? Testing a new framework live with a beta group and asking for their feedback. It wasn't flashy, but it was real. And more importantly, it gave his brain a new reference point: risk doesn't always lead to regret. Sometimes, it leads to progress.

Perfectionism as Protection

Patti is the person who makes things look effortless. She's the one who arrives early, color-codes her planner, double-checks her emails, and always seems two steps ahead. Her work is meticulous. Her standards are sky-high. But behind the scenes, she's stuck in a cycle where perfectionism refuses to let her break.

She's been quietly building a personal development workshop series. She's passionate about it. It aligns with her gifts. She knows it could make a difference. But every time she gets close to sharing it with the world, she edits herself out of it. One more tweak. One more test run. One more round of revisions. And then maybe, she'll feel ready.

What Patti doesn't realize is that her perfectionism isn't just about high standards. It's about fear. Fear that she'll be exposed if she shows up as anything less than flawless. Disappointed. Misunderstood. And because her brain has stored any past criticism as threat signals, it whispers to her: "Don't risk it. Make it better first."

The emotional load of carrying that kind of vigilance is draining. Decision fatigue sets in. Every creative task becomes emotionally charged. So, her brain responds with avoidance, not because she doesn't care, but because the cost of imperfection feels too high.

Her shift came when she stopped tying her value to the outcome and started practicing exposure in safe doses. Her first micro-bold move? She hosted a pilot episode for the series, even though the scripting wasn't fully fleshed out. And when nothing bad happened, when her viewers actually affirmed her voice and vision, her brain got a new message; a message that "done" is powerful. Shared is sacred. Imperfection isn't dangerous, it's human.

The Fear of Being Seen

Alex is full of vision. Their journals are bursting with ideas, creative sketches, program outlines, business names. They light up when talking about their goals, until it's time to actually take the first step. Then the light dims. The voice of doubt gets louder. And the idea goes back into the notebook, locked behind the phrase, "Not yet."

Alex doesn't struggle with creativity. They struggle with exposure. Deep down, boldness feels like visibility, and visibility feels like risk. As someone who grew up in environments where blending in was safer than standing out, their nervous system has learned to equate forward movement with emotional danger.

So when boldness calls, Alex hesitates. Not because they don't care. But because their body says, "Play it safe." Better to almost start than to start and be seen. Better to keep dreaming than risk being misunderstood.

But like Overton and Patti, Alex reached a point where staying stuck was more painful than the fear of moving. Their first micro-bold move? Naming their idea out loud to someone they trusted. No pitch deck. No social media post. Just a quiet confession to someone who could hold space without judgment. And in doing so, Alex's brain got the message: speaking the dream doesn't make you unsafe. It makes you real.

The Domino Effect of Micro-Boldness

By now, you've seen how Overton, Patti, and Alex each carry their own version of stuckness – overthinking, perfectionism, and almost-starting-but underneath it all, the same truth remains: their brains, like yours and mine, are wired to protect before they pursue. That protective wiring often shows up as hesitation, procrastination, or "I'll do it when I'm more ready." But readiness rarely shows up on its own. Boldness isn't born out of waiting but out of movement.

Here's the good news: you don't need a huge breakthrough to move forward. You don't need to suddenly become a different person or have the perfect plan in place. What you need is a shift. A moment. A move. That's where The Domino Effect of Micro-Boldness comes in.

When you tip the first domino and take one brave, imperfect action, you activate a cascade of momentum. It might feel small at first. So small that you're tempted to dismiss it. But science tells us that even small actions can rewire neural patterns and train your brain to stop defaulting to fear. Each small move disrupts the mental loop that says, "I can't do this," and instead creates a new one: "I can take one step."

Think of it like muscle memory. The more often you engage your boldness muscle, especially through low-stakes, everyday decisions, the more familiar it becomes. The less power fear holds. Eventually, your brain starts to expect action instead of retreat. And from there, everything begins to shift.

Let me paint a picture.

When I first started leading my team through micro-bold moves during the belonging moment in our staff meetings, I wasn't just trying to get people to take initiative; I was helping them retrain how they saw themselves. I watched colleagues who used to avoid difficult conversations begin speaking up more confidently. One team member who struggled to present ideas started leading our client meetings. It didn't happen because we did something flashy. It happened because we practiced small acts of courage until they became normal.

Overton did the same thing when he decided to email a mentor instead of over-researching what "networking" should look like. Patti did it when she published the first blog post with a typo she would've previously agonized over. Alex? They said yes to hosting a community meeting with only 10 people signed up and walked away energized to do it again.

That's the domino effect in motion. And once you start? It becomes harder not to keep going. Now let's put it into practice.

This exercise isn't meant to feel heavy. In fact, the lighter it feels, the more likely you are to follow through. This is about getting your brain used to the sensation of moving—not perfectly, but consistently.

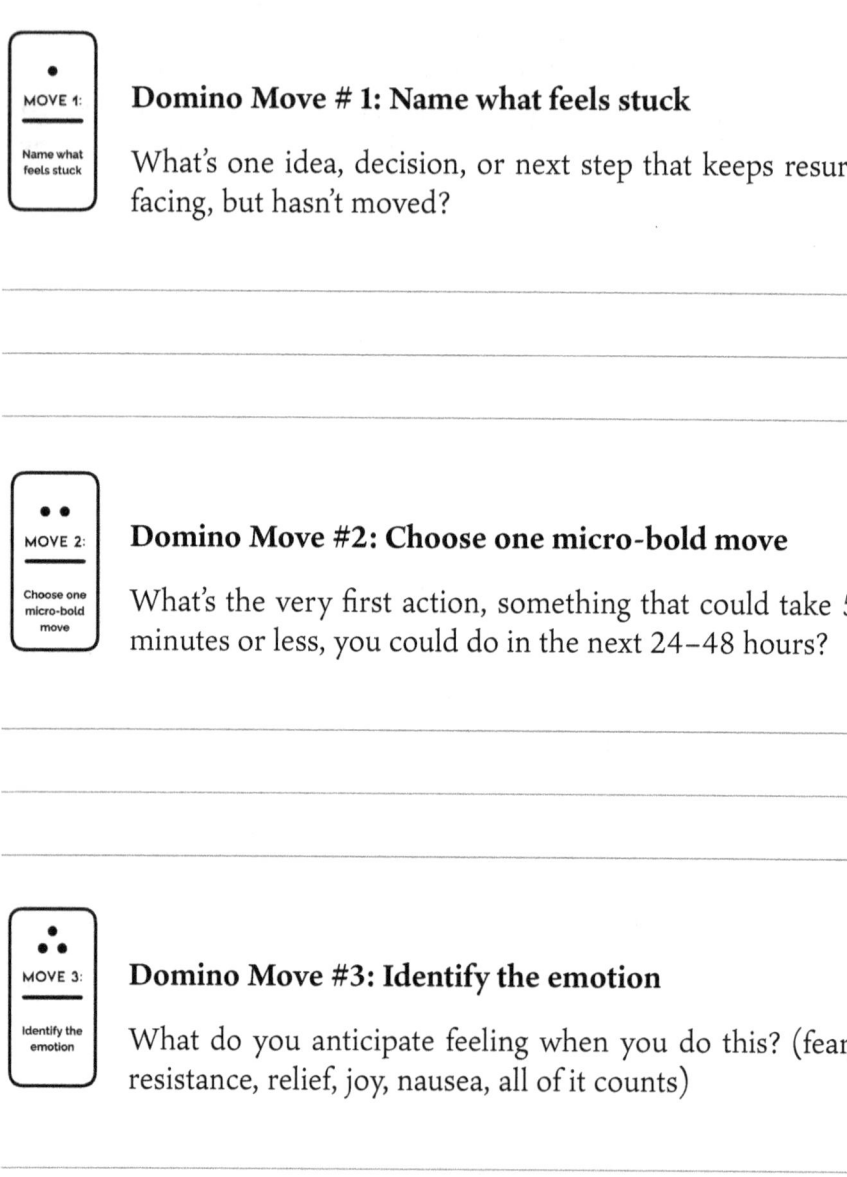

Domino Move # 1: Name what feels stuck

What's one idea, decision, or next step that keeps resurfacing, but hasn't moved?

Domino Move #2: Choose one micro-bold move

What's the very first action, something that could take 5 minutes or less, you could do in the next 24–48 hours?

Domino Move #3: Identify the emotion

What do you anticipate feeling when you do this? (fear, resistance, relief, joy, nausea, all of it counts)

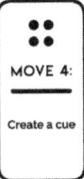

Domino Move #4: Create a cue

What will you pair this with, so it becomes part of your daily rhythm? (Example: "After I make my morning coffee, I'll take my micro-bold move.")

_____

_____

_____

Domino Move #5: Anchor your why

Write down why this matters to you, even in a small way. Write down what's at stake if you don't move. Post those answers somewhere that you'll see them often.

_____

_____

_____

Pro Tip: The power of the domino effect is in its consistency, not its intensity. Don't let urgency trick you into thinking bigger is better. You're not trying to prove something, you're trying to rewire something. Build a pattern that reminds your brain: "I move forward now."

#MOVEANYWAY

You've just uncovered one of the most important truths about boldness: it's not something you're missing; it's something your brain is learning. And like any skill, it takes repetition, compassion, and small but steady effort. The fear that's been holding you back? It isn't a flaw in your character. It's a signal from your nervous system trying to keep you safe. But safety and stagnation are not the same. Growth requires discomfort, and courage is built in the tension between where you are and where you're called to go.

So now that you know how your mind works, the question becomes: What will you teach it next? Will you let it continue rehearsing fear, or will you begin showing it what progress feels like, even if it's just one step at a time? That's where your power lives, not in waiting for the fear to go away, but in moving anyway, knowing you're rewiring something ancient in service of something extraordinary.

As you close out this chapter, take a moment to anchor what you've learned. The following statement of truth is your reminder to speak this affirmation out loud, and the journal prompt is your space to process, explore, and get honest about where you are and where you're ready to go. Let this be the start of your rewiring, one micro-bold move at a time.

Statement of truth:

My brain remembers fear, but I'm teaching it courage, one bold move at a time. Whenever I act courageously, I rewire my brain to choose boldness over fear.

Journal Prompt

Where in your life are you waiting for clarity, perfection, or confidence before making a move? What's one micro-bold decision you can make today that could activate your own domino effect?

Chapter 2

THE LIE OF A PERFECT START

You're waiting for a green light that doesn't exist...because you think you need a flawless beginning.

There is a myth many of us have lived by for far too long: that the conditions have to be perfect before we begin. That clarity comes before courage. That readiness will tap us on the shoulder and tell us the exact moment to boldly move. But that moment? It rarely comes the way we imagine it. The stars don't align. The road doesn't clear. And yet, we keep waiting, not because we lack ideas, but because we've bought into the lie that boldness needs a perfect beginning.

In this context, perfectionism isn't about clean desks or color-coded calendars. It's about postponing movement until we feel invincible. It disguises itself as wisdom, preparation, or excellence. But behind the scenes, its fear wearing a very professional outfit. And it's keeping too many of us from taking the very first step.

Let's be honest, perfectionism has range. It sounds like, "I just want to do it right." It feels like endlessly tweaking your website before you share it. It shows up as asking for one more opinion, doing one more round of edits, and then one more. It tells us that getting it wrong will be irreversible, that our credibility hinges on flawlessness, and that we'll only be taken seriously if everything looks polished from day one.

But here's the catch: perfect is a moving target. By the time you think you've reached it, the goalposts have shifted. The truth is what we really fear is judgment. We convince ourselves that starting small is risky, that launching imperfectly will somehow disqualify us, or worse, embarrass us. So we stay in planning mode. We workshop the idea to death. We wait until the timing feels "right," until the branding feels "on point," until the confidence magically arrives. And often, underneath all that waiting is one root fear: what will people say? We picture critics. We imagine high school friends lurking online. We hear the imaginary group chat already talking. But as KevOnStage – comedian, creator, and king of keeping it real – once said on a social media reel, "Okay, let's say they do talk about you. Let's say they call it weird. So what? That's it. It happened. That was the worst of it. Now what?" His point? Their judgment isn't enough to stop you, unless you give it that kind of power. And you don't have to.

We're scared of being seen starting small, misunderstood, or making a visible mistake. But the only way to build something that matters is to begin, messy and all. The truth is, there's no such thing as a flawless beginning. Every dream you admire, every business you follow, every story that inspired you, none of them started perfectly. They started anyway. The myth of the perfect start keeps us sitting on brilliant ideas, silencing our creativity, and stalling progress. But the moment you decide that messy movement matters more than immaculate planning? That's when things finally shift. Because movement isn't just what gets you unstuck, it rewires your brain to believe that progress is possible, even when perfection isn't.

No Map. No Real Plan. Just A Nudge!

We've discussed how the perfect start myth holds people back. But it's one thing to understand it, and another to live it. I know this trap personally. I've wrestled with the voice that says, "Wait until it all makes sense," and the part of me that fears what might happen if I leap without knowing where I'll land. But sometimes, clarity doesn't come before the move. It comes because of the move.

When I decided to move to Dallas, everything about the decision felt imperfect. I didn't have a job lined up. I didn't have family there. I wasn't moving with a partner or a clear roadmap. All I had was a deep knowing that something needed to shift, that staying in place was slowly draining the version of me I wanted to become.

It was one of those decisions that looked reckless on paper but felt absolutely necessary in my spirit. And I wrestled with it. Shouldn't I wait until I have more savings? More certainty? A clear offer letter in hand? But the longer I stayed still, the more I realized that perfection wasn't coming to rescue me. I had to make the move first. So I did. I trusted that clarity would meet me on the road.

That decision changed everything. Not because Dallas handed me a silver platter of success, but because I proved to myself that I could move without a full map. That imperfect beginnings still count. That momentum is a decision, not a circumstance. My Dallas moves taught me something I've carried with me ever since: forward motion doesn't wait for perfection; it responds to intention. By choosing to go, I interrupted the pattern of waiting for life to happen to me and instead began creating life with purpose. It showed me that boldness isn't about having every answer, it's about being willing to say yes anyway. And if I could make one imperfect decision and still land on my feet, maybe other bold moves didn't need to be perfect either; they just needed to be honest, aligned, and in motion.

When Perfectionism Pretends to Be Preparation

My decision to move didn't come with a blueprint, and that's exactly what made it bold. But not everyone's stuck point looks like a cross-country leap. For some, the fear isn't about moving to a new city, it's about sharing a new idea, speaking up, or starting something that feels deeply personal. That's where Patti comes in. Patti's story reminds us that perfectionism doesn't just delay progress; it convinces us we're not allowed to begin until we've earned the right to try.

Remember, Patti is our stereotypical Type A planner, the prepper, the one with color-coded vision boards and a million half-finished Google Docs. Her mind was a vault of brilliant ideas, but her boldness never made it past the editing stage. If Chapter 1 helped us understand the fear behind her hesitation, this chapter is about her quiet rebellion against it.

Patti had spent nearly two years refining a workshop series for women navigating confidence and career transitions. She had done everything except launch it. Each time she neared the starting line, a new reason appeared to postpone, one more credential to earn, a better bio, sleeker visuals, a new font that felt "just right." She told herself she was being responsible, waiting for the right time to present her best work to the world.

But what was really happening? Her brain had created a false contract: Don't show up until you're flawless. And beneath that was a deeper fear—that if she was visible before she was perfect, she'd be judged, criticized, or rejected. Her nervous system wasn't just delaying a project but protecting her from perceived emotional harm.

Then something shifted.

One evening, after reviewing her notes for the hundredth time, Patti asked herself a hard question: What's actually scarier, sharing something imperfect, or never sharing it at all? And for the first time, the silence felt heavier than the risk. That moment cracked something open. Her micro-bold move wasn't flashy or grand. She invited five women to a virtual preview session. No polished deck. No final logo. Just her voice, her story, and a few questions that had lived in her heart for far too long. The conversation was raw and beautiful. No one asked about branding or bios. They leaned in. They listened. And they told her afterward that it was exactly what they needed.

That one imperfect step rewired something in Patti's brain. Not because it erased her fear, but because it gave her new evidence. It reminded her that her worth wasn't tied to polish. That value lives in the doing, not just the preparing. And more than anything, it taught her this: action doesn't just create momentum—it reshapes your belief in what's possible.

Patti's story matters because so many of us are carrying bold ideas inside of us that are getting delayed, not by laziness, but by perfectionism dressed up as preparation. The first draft doesn't have to be the final draft. It just has to exist. And the sooner we let go of the myth of a flawless beginning, the sooner we get to experience the freedom that comes from starting anyway.

And Then There's The Other Two...

While Patti's journey with perfectionism may feel familiar, she's not the only one who's struggled with the myth of a flawless beginning.

Overton, our resident overthinker, doesn't usually wrestle with "if" he should take a bold step. He's stuck in the loop of "how". His brain spins out 15 different scenarios and risk profiles before he even opens a blank page. By the time he's mapped out every potential obstacle, the window of opportunity has passed - and his confidence along with it.

For Overton, it's not fear of failure, it's fear of not being fully prepared. He convinces himself that he'll act once he has more time, research, or a more detailed plan. But what Overton's starting to learn is that certainty doesn't precede action. It follows it. His turning point came when he forced himself to take one messy step forward – before finishing the spreadsheet, before reading another book – and realized the world didn't collapse. He didn't need the full plan. He just needed a starting point.

Alex, on the other hand, is the almost-starter. Their superpower is vision – the big, bold, creative visions. But they've spent years stuck in the starting gate, waiting for the perfect opening. The "one day" list keeps growing, and while Alex tells themselves they're just waiting for the right time, deep down they know time isn't the issue.

What really holds Alex back is the pressure to prove that starting something means they'll see it through flawlessly. So instead of trying and risking the messiness of trial and error, they stop short. They linger in the land of possibility, where nothing can fail, but nothing gets built either.

But recently, something small shifted. Alex decided to put one of their ideas into action—a community art event in their neighborhood; without a budget, committee, or formal sponsor. They invited neighbors through a group text, printed flyers at the library, and hosted it in a borrowed backyard. And people came. Kids painted. Adults shared stories. And Alex realized: the goal isn't to get it right on day one. It's to get it going.

Why A Strategic Start Is Necessary

So why do we hold back when something new is calling us forward?

The need for a "perfect start" is less about preparation and more about protection. Perfectionism feels like planning, but at its core, it's your brain trying to shield you from emotional risk. Let's be honest: telling yourself to "just start" when your mind is spiraling through doubt, over analysis, or fear rarely works. In fact, it often backfires. What your brain needs isn't more inspiration; it needs a strategy. This is where science steps in.

Psychologists refer to anticipatory anxiety as the brain's tendency to rehearse future failure in advance. Your mind scans for potential threats, running simulations of what could go wrong. It's not trying to sabotage you; it's trying to keep you safe. But safety and stagnation often go hand in hand. You can't build a bold life if your brain only knows how to protect you from discomfort.

Psychologist Peter Gollwitzer introduced the concept of implementation intentions, a research-backed strategy for turning vague goals into specific action. His work shows that when people create a simple "if-then" plan – stating when, where, and how they'll act – they're far more likely to follow through, even when self-doubt or distractions arise.[2] These mini-contracts with your brain give your

---

2. Gollwitzer, Peter. (1999). Implementation Intentions: Strong Effects of Simple Plans. American Psychologist. 54. 493-503. 10.1037/0003-066X.54.7.493

nervous system something to anchor. They don't eliminate fear but make movement possible, even when perfectionism is whispering in your ear.

Too many options can also stall us out. Psychologist Barry Schwartz explains in his widely viewed TED Talk on the Paradox of Choice that an overload of options, especially when paired with high expectations, can lead to paralysis.[3] If you're constantly refining an idea or stalling until it's "right," your brain becomes overwhelmed by potential outcomes and avoids action altogether.

And there's more.

An article by psychologists Fuschia M. Sirois and Timothy A. Pychyl, titled "Procrastination and the Priority of Short-Term Mood Regulation" explains that procrastination, especially for perfectionists, is less about laziness and more about avoiding discomfort.[4] We delay not because we're unmotivated, but because we're trying to protect our current emotional state, even at the expense of our future self.

That's the lie of the perfect start: if you wait a little longer, it'll get easier.

But science and experience, tell a different story.

You don't reduce fear by thinking your way through it. You reduce fear by proving to your brain that forward is safe. The only thing that builds momentum is movement. And that's exactly why the next activity isn't about vision boards or elaborate goal setting. It's about giving your brain a new reference point—a moment of imperfect action it can look back on as evidence that messy starts still count, and imperfect motion still moves mountains.

---

3. Barry Schwartz, "The Paradox of Choice," TED Talk, 2005.
4. Fuschia M. Sirois and Timothy A. Pychyl, "Procrastination and the Priority of Short-Term Mood Regulation: Consequences for Future Self," Social and Personality Psychology Compass, vol. 7, no. 2 (2013): 115–127.

Let's Put These Strategies into Practice

The Start Anyway Script™

The Start Anyway Script™ is a neuroscience-backed exercise designed to interrupt the perfectionism loop. You'll identify your delay patterns, write a specific micro-action plan using Gollwitzer's formula, and commit to doing something before it's perfect. Inspired by Gollwitzer's research on implementation intentions and Schwartz's work on decision paralysis, this tool helps you break through hesitation by scripting a real-time action plan.

Step 1: Call out the delay loop (write down the project, decision, or desire you've been putting off."

+ Example: I've been delaying _____, because I keep telling myself _____.

Step 2: Rewire with an Implementation Intention (use this sentence structure to prime your brain for bold action)

+ Example: If it's [day/time], and I'm in [place/situation], then I will [micro-bold action] – even if it's not perfect. (e.g. If it's Tuesday at 10 am, and I'm at my desk, then I will send the draft email to my client – even if it's not perfect.)

Replace The Lie

Step 1: Name the idea (Write down one thing you've been delaying because it "wasn't ready yet.")

Step 2: List the lies (List 3–5 thoughts that have kept you from starting. These are the "perfect start" lies your brain has repeated.)

Step 3: Replace them with truths (Now rewrite each lie with a truth that affirms imperfect action.)

Example

Lie	Replaced Truth
• I need a website before I can start	• I can start with what I have. The website can come later.
• No one will take me seriously without credentials	• People connect with authenticity, not polish
• I need more time/money/confidence	• I don't need to be fearless; I just need to be willing.

Step 4: Fill in the Staircase (On each level of the stairs, write down a bold step you can take towards one of your replaced statements of truth.

#MOVEANYWAY

Now that you've permitted yourself to begin, with clarity about what matters, what's noise, and what you're claiming as *enough*, let's ground this chapter with one final shift. Because boldness isn't about a one-time move; it's about how you train your mind to believe that movement is always possible. You don't need a flawless beginning to build something meaningful. The lie of the perfect start is persuasive, but it's not your truth. You were not called to wait for certainty. You were called to walk in faith, to move even when the outline isn't clear. Because what you start today doesn't have to be permanent. It just has to be real. And once it's real, it can grow.

This is your moment. And it doesn't have to be perfect. It only has to be yours.

Let's anchor what you've uncovered with a statement of truth you can carry forward, and a journal prompt to help you make sense of what's stirring beneath the surface.

Statement of truth:

I release the myth of the flawless beginning. My progress is not waiting for perfection. It begins the moment I decide to move.

Journal Prompt

What are you waiting for permission to begin? What would change if you allowed yourself to start with what you have now?

_____

_____

_____

_____

_____

Chapter 3

THE ILLUSION OF CONTROL: WHEN COMPARISON BECOMES THE COMPASS

When you hand the compass to comparison, don't be surprised if you end up lost. Control is comforting, but it won't take you anywhere new.

There's a particular kind of stuckness that doesn't always come with flashing warning signs. It's not the kind that announces itself with panic or paralysis. It's quieter. More cunning. Sometimes, it slides in subtly, masked as admiration, hidden in inspiration, wrapped in someone else's highlight reel. It sneaks in under the surface, disguised as diligence, disguised as discernment. But really? It's just distraction wearing a thoughtful expression.

Comparison doesn't always show up in dramatic moments. Sometimes it arrives in the middle of a seemingly ordinary day. You're feeling good, maybe even proud of something you've built or planned, until you scroll past someone else doing something similar. Suddenly, what felt promising now feels inadequate. The excitement fades. The clarity blurs. And a voice creeps in: "Well, they already did it. And probably better."

It's rarely loud. More often, comparison whispers. Behind a friend's compliment. Behind a colleague's success story. Behind that well-meaning "you've got this" from someone who already seems to have it all figured out. The voice doesn't always tell you to quit. It just tells you to wait. To tweak. To polish. To not embarrass yourself by showing up before it's perfect.

But here's what's dangerous about comparison: it doesn't just distort your confidence. For many of us, comparison isn't about envy, it's about direction. When you're uncertain about where you're headed, it's tempting to use someone else's journey as your GPS. You follow their path. You mimic their pacing. You assume their version is the safer bet. And without realizing it, your bold move becomes a watered-down echo of someone else's story. You stop building the thing that was true to you and start chasing what seems to be working for them. You start editing your voice to sound more like theirs. You shrink your idea into something more digestible. Safer. Familiar. You lose the plot, not because you weren't capable, but because you let someone else's story rewrite your own.

And when that spiral starts, control is never far behind.

Craving control is often just fear with a better PR team. Because if you can't be the best, you tell yourself at least you'll be polished. If you can't go first, you'll at least go the safest route. If you can't guarantee applause, you'll hold out for a less risky moment. Control becomes your coping mechanism. You rework the outline. You change the goal. You micromanage every outcome until the idea no longer breathes. And the irony? The more you try to perfect it, the more disconnected you feel from it. You keep telling yourself that all of the undoing & redoing is a smart strategy. But what you're really doing is stalling. Because if you can't guarantee success, you'll try to guarantee the outcome. That's how control works – it seduces you into believing that more planning means less risk. It promises protection but often delivers paralysis.

And beneath all of it? The craving for certainty, that desire to know it will work. That longing to feel like the risk will be rewarded. That secret hope that if we play it safe long enough, we'll be able to skip the vulnerable parts. That deep, familiar ache for assurance that this thing will work before you commit. That your effort won't be wasted. That if you take a leap, there's a safety net, preferably branded, budgeted, and co-signed by someone with a larger platform than yours. We don't just want clarity. We want a contract with success before we ever put ourselves out there.

But here's the truth you already know in your bones: boldness doesn't come with guarantees. It comes with gut checks. With shaky yeses. With trying, not knowing, and still choosing to move. You don't get to build something brave while avoiding uncertainty. You don't get to change your life without being willing to risk looking un-polished or feeling unsure. Clarity doesn't always come first. Cour-age does.

This chapter is about the invisible anchors that keep us from mov-ing forward, the urge to compare, the obsession with control, the myth of certainty. These are the habits that convince us we're being smart, strategic, and careful. But often, we're just being scared. And if we don't name them, we start letting them decide on our behalf.

So, before we talk about how to move anyway, we need to ask the hard question: What's really behind the delay? Whose voice(s) are you letting drive? And what would happen if you reclaimed your compass and pointed it back toward the truth?

The Cost of Watching Too Long

Before we dive into the stories that bring this chapter to life, I want you to pause. Not just mentally, but physically. Go stand in front of a mirror. Yes, an actual mirror. Look at yourself. Really look. Because what's been keeping you stuck might not just be the comparisons you make, the control you crave, or the certainty you've been waiting for. What's been keeping you stuck might also be that somewhere along the way, you stopped seeing yourself.

Too often, we get so caught up watching other people, tracking their pace, progress, and polish, that we lose sight of our own voice and value. We tell ourselves we're just gathering inspiration. Just do-ing research. Just learning. But there comes a point where observing becomes a form of hiding. The cost of watching too long isn't always immediate. It's slow, subtle, and slippery. It chips away at your confidence one scroll, one comparison, one moment of second-guessing at a time.

So, here's what I want you to do. As you stand in front of that mirror, take a breath and ask yourself these three questions out loud:

1. What idea or dream have I put on hold because someone else already did something similar?

2. Whose journey am I tracking so closely that I've blurred the edges of my own?

3. What has it cost me, mentally, emotionally, creatively, to keep waiting for a "better" version of myself to show up before I act?

Say the answers out loud. Not just in your head. Let your own voice be the one that tells the truth.

Let yourself see what it's cost you to keep delaying your bold move. Let yourself hear the voice that's been buried under all the noise.

This isn't about guilt. It's about awareness. Because once you see the pattern, you get to interrupt it.

You don't need to journal this unless something inside you wants to write. But you do need to notice. You need to witness what's been happening underneath the surface so that the stories you'll read next don't just feel familiar, they feel freeing.

Now that you've taken a moment to meet yourself in the mirror, let's explore how these invisible habits, comparison, control, and craving certainty, have shown up in the lives of three people you've already met. Their stories might just help you name something you've been carrying, too.

When the Compass Points Elsewhere

Research Can Be a Stumbling Block

Overton had always been the go-to guy for problem solving. He could build a framework in his sleep, had bookmarks full of strategy blogs, and kept multiple whiteboards filled with plans he hadn't shared with anyone. Planning made him feel powerful. But what looked like productivity on the outside was actually paralysis in disguise.

He had been dreaming of launching a leadership coaching practice for over a year. The concept was solid. The audience was clear. He even had a few test clients in mind. But instead of starting, Overton buried himself in more prep, books, market research, and hypothetical "what ifs." He told himself he was being responsible, but deep down, he knew he was hiding. Overthinking gave him a sense of control in a space where clarity was anything but guaranteed.

It wasn't until a friend challenged him, "You don't need another template. You need to take the first step," that something shifted. Overton decided to host a low-key coaching circle on Zoom for a few trusted colleagues. No fancy graphics. No full branding. Just him, his voice, and the content he already knew. And something amazing happened: they loved it. Not because it was flashy, but because it was real. After that, he couldn't deny the truth; he didn't need more information. He needed more trust in his ability to figure it out on the way.

Polish ≠ Perfect

Back in Chapter 2, Patti made her first micro-bold move by launching a preview workshop before she felt fully ready. It was raw, unpolished, and it resonated. That small step gave her a taste of what was possible when she stopped hiding behind perfection. But growth isn't linear. And neither is boldness.

Patti had a bigger vision this time: a digital series on redefining professional identity for women in mid-career pivots. She knew the stories women weren't telling. She knew the language that would resonate. And she had a solid outline for the first six episodes.

But the launch? It kept getting delayed.

First, it was the lighting. Then the intro music. Then she decided to revise the title sequence... again. She told herself she was "raising the bar," aiming for excellence. But what she was really doing was moving the goalposts. Her Trello board was full, task after task labeled "refine," "re-record," or "tweak." None of them said "post."

Patti didn't realize it yet, but her need to perfect every detail wasn't about quality. It was about control. She had started comparing her concept to digital creators with sleek branding and major sponsorships. She convinced herself that anything less than flawless would make her look like she didn't belong. And underneath that fear? The same vulnerability she faced before, this time dressed in a more "professional" disguise.

Then one evening, a former mentee sent her a voice note: "I wish more women like you talked about this stuff. Everyone's so polished. I just want real." The message hit Patti in her gut. She realized she was trying to protect a brand that hadn't even been born yet—building walls around something no one had even seen.

So she gave herself a deadline. One weekend. One episode. No more edits. She filmed the first segment using natural light from her window, her iPhone propped up by cookbooks, and the exact outline she'd written months ago. And then, she hit publish.

It wasn't perfect. But it was powerful. Comments rolled in. Women said they finally felt seen. That they weren't alone, that someone had found the words they hadn't been able to say out loud. For Patti, that first episode wasn't just a launch but a reckoning. A return to what mattered. A reminder that her voice never needed permission, it just needed space.

She didn't need more polish. She needed to trust that her message was already enough.

Afraid of Missing "The Moment"

Alex had been sitting on a tech-for-social-good idea for over a year; a mobile app designed to connect grassroots organizers with local volunteers. But every time they revisited it, the self-doubt grew louder. "It's already been done." "There are better coders." "You don't have the funding or the network." They weren't scrolling through social media for inspiration anymore; they were scrolling for evidence that they were too late.

The deeper truth? Alex wasn't afraid their idea wouldn't work. They were afraid that they wouldn't be the one to make it work. That someone else had already claimed the market. That their voice didn't matter in the crowded noise.

Eventually, what shifted for Alex wasn't clarity or funding; it was exhaustion. They were tired of talking themselves out of things. Tired of building a dream in theory but never letting it breathe. So, they put together a rough prototype using free tools, pitched it to a local startup incubator, and landed a spot in a community accelerator.

That wasn't the final destination; it was the first step. For the first time, Alex saw that boldness wasn't about being first or being best. It was about being true. To the idea. To the need. To themselves.

These three aren't just fictional composites, they're stories and reflections of real patterns I've witnessed repeatedly. Maybe you saw yourself in their stories. Maybe you've lived a version of all three. I certainly have.

And while their breakthrough moments are real and beautiful, I'd be lying if I said I didn't still wrestle with these same anchors. Comparison, control, and certainty don't disappear the moment you gain awareness. But awareness gives you a choice. A new response. A different script.

In the next section, I want to take you into one of my own moments, where I had to face the temptation to shrink, edit, or delay simply because I didn't know how it would all work out. It's a story I haven't shared often, but it changed the way I define progress and boldness. And maybe, just maybe, it will give you permission to do the same.

When I Almost Talked Myself Out of the Room

I've lived versions of Overton, Patti, and Alex more times than I can count. But there's one story I rarely share, mostly because, for a long time, I felt embarrassed by it. I should've known better. I do this work. I teach people how to move through fear and stop waiting for perfection. But boldness isn't something you teach once and master forever. It's a choice you keep making, especially in moments when it would be easier to hide.

I was invited to speak on a national stage a few years ago. It was the kind of opportunity I had dreamed about: hundreds of people in the audience, a room full of leaders and decision-makers, and the freedom to shape the message however I wanted. I should've been excited, and I was. But as the date got closer, something shifted. Instead of preparing with confidence, I started second-guessing every single thing.

I rewrote the talk three times. I researched other speakers. I watched their reels, studied their stage presence, and started wondering if I should mimic their style. Their cadence. Their tone. I even changed my outfit plan one day because it didn't "look like a keynote speaker." I convinced myself that my message wouldn't land if I didn't appear in the right packaging.

And underneath all of that? I didn't like the way I looked. I wasn't at my ideal weight or size, not even close. At the time, I didn't yet know that a medical condition was playing a major role in my body's changes. All I knew was that I didn't feel like myself. I felt heavy, uncomfortable, and deeply self-conscious.

On top of that, I had just experienced a painful rejection in a relationship that left me questioning my worth in ways I hadn't fully acknowledged. The thought of being seen on stage, really seen, felt unbearable. I didn't want to face more rejection, especially not in front of a crowd. Not when I already felt so far from my best.

It sounds small. But when you're caught in that spiral, it feels like self-preservation. What I didn't realize at the time was that I wasn't preparing, I was performing for a version of "success" that wasn't even mine. I was trying to control the outcome by molding myself into something that looked safer. And behind that need for control? Fear. Fear of not being enough. Fear of failing publicly. Fear of being seen and still not chosen.

Two nights before the event, I had a breakdown. Quiet tears. Spiraling thoughts. A deep desire to back out and tell them I was no longer available. And then, something in me paused. I asked myself a question I now return to often: "If I showed up fully as myself and it still wasn't enough; would I still be proud of how I showed up?"

That question unraveled something. I didn't magically gain confidence. I didn't suddenly believe I was the best speaker in the lineup. But I remembered who I was. I remembered the stories I'd already lived, the rooms I'd already transformed, the people whom my voice had moved. And I remembered that my job wasn't to be the best. My job was to be true.

So I wore what I planned to wear. I delivered the talk I originally wrote. I stood on that stage and told the truth, even when my hands were shaking. And when it was over? People didn't come up to me because I was the most polished. They came because I was the most real.

That experience changed how I define readiness. It reminded me that certainty doesn't come from outcomes, it comes from alignment. From choosing to trust your voice, even when your fear is louder than your confidence. From recognizing that shrinking yourself to match someone else's success story will never lead you to your own. I share this not because I've mastered it, but because I know what it costs to delay your dreams in the name of perfection. And I know what it feels like to finally move, even with the fear still whispering.

What I didn't realize at the time was that I wasn't preparing, I was performing for a version of "success" that wasn't even mine. I had let comparison and fear distort the truth of who I was. And yet, even in that moment of insecurity, God hadn't changed His mind about me. "I praise You because I am fearfully and wonderfully made" (Psalm 139:14 NIV) isn't just a verse we quote when we feel confident; it's a reminder for the moments we don't. The moments when we feel unseen, unworthy, or unsure. That verse became my anchor. I realized I had been spending so much time trying to meet the world's standards that I had forgotten I was already created with intention, already equipped, already chosen.

So as we move into the next section, I want to bring both my faith and the science into the conversation. Because I believe God gave us both truth and tools. And when used together, they can help us silence the noise, see ourselves more clearly, and finally start moving forward, with grace, strategy, and the kind of boldness rooted in something deeper than applause.

The Lie of Lack and the Trap of Control: Why We Stay Stuck

If comparison is the whisper, then scarcity is the echo, a low hum of doubt that convinces you there's not enough room, time, or validation to go around. And that echo grows louder in a digital world where curated success is always a scroll away.

A higher education research study conducted with university students found that people who frequently engaged in social media comparison were more likely to experience imposter feelings, emotional burnout, and task avoidance, especially on personal growth goals.[5] Interestingly, the study noted that the cause wasn't a lack of skill. It was cognitive overload and lowered self-belief, a mental fog that forms when you spend more time watching than doing.

This is the hidden cost of staying stuck: your capacity to act shrinks the longer you let comparison dictate your pace. And it doesn't stop there.

---

5. Whelan, Eoin and Islam, Najmul and Brooks, Stoney, The Effects of Social Media Overload on Academic Performance (December 4, 2019)
Vogel, Erin & Rose, Jason & Roberts, Lindsay & Eckles, Katheryn. (2014). Social Comparison, Social Media, and Self-Esteem. Psychology of Popular Media Culture. 3. 206-222. 10.1037/ppm0000047

When self-doubt builds, scarcity steps in. You tell yourself there's only one seat at the table, and someone else already took it. You hesitate to move because it feels like the market's too crowded, the moment's already passed, or you don't bring anything "new" to the table. But this scarcity mindset doesn't just affect your emotions. It literally impacts your executive functioning, how you make decisions, assess risk, and engage with opportunity.

A study published in *Science* found that people who experience financial, emotional, or time-based scarcity suffer a measurable drop in cognitive function.[6] It narrows our focus to short-term survival and self-protection, limiting our creativity and making us more reactive than proactive.

Scarcity makes you hyper-aware of what's missing instead of what's possible. You hesitate to share your ideas because they're not "fully formed." You talk yourself out of the first step because someone else already seems to be five steps ahead. You wait for conditions to be just right, even if that day never comes.

So how do we disrupt this pattern?

Strategies That Break The Cycle

Conduct Abundance Audits

When scarcity thinking creeps in, the goal isn't to drown it in fake positivity. The goal is to remind your brain that you are not empty-handed. Try this: conduct an Abundance Audit at the end of each week. Write down:

- One resource you already have access to (time, tools, relationships, or experience).

- One thing you've learned this week that made you better prepared.

- And one person you could reach out to for support or insight.

---

6. Shah, A. K., Mullainathan, S., & Shafir, E. (2012). Some consequences of having too little. Science, 338(6107), 682–685. https://doi.org/10.1126/science.1222426

This practice helps your brain shift from what's missing to what's already available and reminds you that progress is still within reach.

Scarcity also thrives when we tie our worth to outcomes. That's where control tries to take over. When we can't guarantee success, we try to guarantee safety. We delay, revise, and over-prepare under the guise of being "strategic," but what we're really doing is avoiding vulnerability.

Brené Brown's research on vulnerability reframes this: she defines it not as weakness, but as risk, uncertainty, and emotional exposure, the exact conditions required for creativity and breakthrough.[7] You don't build something bold by minimizing all risk; you build it by increasing your capacity to navigate discomfort.

Build A Stretch Space

If control is your coping mechanism, create what I call a Stretch Space, a weekly window (even 30 minutes) where you commit to doing something imperfect, in public. That might be sharing a rough idea, asking for feedback before something's polished, or publishing a first draft. The goal isn't exposure for exposure's sake, it's resilience training. Every time you show up without all the answers, you're building your ability to move without control, steering the wheel.

And yet, even the best strategies will still leave you wanting something deeper, a reason to keep showing up when you don't feel ready. That's where your faith comes in.

Seen, Known, And Still Chosen

There is a spiritual cost to staying stuck. When we shrink ourselves down in the name of perfection or comparison, we're not just delaying progress; we're quietly doubting the very way we were created.

Ephesians 2:10 NIV reminds us: "For we are God's handiwork, created in Christ Jesus to do good works, which God prepared in

---

7. Brown, B. (2012). Daring Greatly: How the Courage to Be Vulnerable Transforms the Way We Live, Love, Parent, and Lead. Gotham Books.
Brown, B. (2010). The Gifts of Imperfection. Hazelden Publishing.

advance for us to do." In other words, your purpose was never an afterthought. It wasn't assigned after you got the job title, the degree, the funding, or the audience. It was woven into your DNA, before the doubt, before the detours, before you ever had something to compare it to.

Still, most of us struggle to believe we're ready when we don't feel our best. I've felt that before, deeply. Especially when I didn't look the way I wanted to. When my body was heavier than it used to be, my confidence cracked, and the lies felt louder: You're not polished enough. You won't be taken seriously. This isn't the version of you that belongs in the spotlight.

I had also just experienced a personal rejection that left me emotionally bruised. The idea of showing up, visibly, vulnerably, felt unbearable. Why risk being dismissed publicly when I was already questioning my worth privately?

But God does not evaluate us based on curated perfection. He sees beyond the surface. Scripture says, "People look at the outward appearance, but the Lord looks at the heart" (1 Samuel 16:7 ESV). When God called Moses to lead, He didn't choose someone polished or obvious. Moses was an outsider born Hebrew, raised Egyptian, caught between two worlds. He had a stutter. A temper. A complicated past. And yet, God still chose him.

Why? Because God wasn't looking for perfection. He was looking for obedience. He was looking for someone who would move, even with trembling hands and uncertain steps.

When you hesitate because you don't "feel ready," remember this: God already knew what you'd look like, sound like, struggle with, and overcome, and still chose YOU. That truth doesn't erase fear. But it does erase the lie that you need to be more than who you are to be useful.

The 5-Day Detox Plan: Reclaim Your Compass

This isn't just a checklist. It's a mindset reset.

Comparison. Control. Craving certainty. These habits don't just slow you down, they distort your view of yourself and your next step. That's why this five-day plan is designed as a detox. A way to clear out the noise, disrupt your default patterns, and come back home to your truth. This detox isn't about restriction; it's about release. A chance to see yourself again and move from that place.

Each day offers one intentional practice to help you move away from external validation and back toward bold, soul-aligned action. Take it one day at a time or stretch it out if you need to. The goal is progress, not performance.

Day 1: Curate Your Inputs

What you take in daily, on your phone, in your conversations, even in your quiet moments, shapes how you see yourself. So today, I want you to scan your digital world and do some pruning. Unfollow or mute at least 10 accounts or group chats that consistently stir up insecurity, urgency, or the feeling that you're falling behind. Let go of the newsletters or podcast episodes that nudge you toward comparison rather than clarity. You're not unfollowing people, you're unfollowing pressure. Research shows that constant upward comparison, especially on social media, contributes to anxiety, self-doubt, and procrastination.[8] By limiting what triggers the spiral, you're making space to hear your own voice again.

Day 2: Reclaim What's Yours

Instead of defining yourself by who you're not, spend time rediscovering who you are. Write down five specific things that make your approach, story, or voice distinctly yours. Say them aloud. Keep them somewhere visible. This exercise isn't fluff, it's neuroscience. Research on identity-based motivation suggests that affirming your unique value can strengthen your confidence and decrease reliance

8. Wang W, Wang M, Hu Q, Wang P, Lei L, Jiang S. Upward social comparison on mobile social media and depression: The mediating role of envy and the moderating role of marital quality. J Affect Disord. 2020 Jun 1;270:143-149. doi: 10.1016/j.jad.2020.03.173. Epub 2020 Apr 5. PMID: 32339106.
Vogel, Erin & Rose, Jason & Roberts, Lindsay & Eckles, Katheryn. (2014). Social Comparison, Social Media, and Self-Esteem. Psychology of Popular Media Culture. 3. 206-222. 10.1037/ppm0000047

on external validation.[9] You don't need more proof that you belong. You need to remember the truth of what you bring.

Day 3: Practice Imperfection

Today, I want you to take one idea, one draft, one moment, and release it into the world before it feels "ready." Post something. Share a voice memo. Submit a pitch. Send the email. Whatever you've been polishing and tweaking, let it breathe. Our brains often equate vulnerability with danger, which is why we delay sharing our work until it feels flawless. But vulnerability is also the birthplace of connection.[10] You don't grow by waiting for certainty, you grow by allowing yourself to be seen anyway.

Day 4: Break The Scarcity Spell

Comparison thrives in a scarcity mindset, believing that if someone else is shining, there's no light left for you. But that's a lie. Boldness operates from abundance. So today, think of a time when you believed there wasn't room for your voice or version. Write that moment down. Then rewrite it from a lens of truth and abundance. For example, instead of "It's already been done," try "Yes, and my version hasn't." Scarcity tells you the opportunity has passed. Abundance reminds you that timing isn't the same as purpose. God's provision doesn't run on competition; it runs on calling.

Day 5: Say Yes Anyway

Say yes, today! Not because the fear is gone. Not because you've mastered the plan. But because you're done letting uncertainty make your decisions for you. Pick one small action that feels bold and

9. Oyserman, D., Bybee, D., & Terry, K. (2006). Possible selves and academic outcomes: How and when possible selves impel action. Journal of Personality and Social Psychology, 91(1), 188–204. https://doi.org/10.1037/0022-3514.91.1.188

Steele, C. M. (1988). The psychology of self-affirmation: Sustaining the integrity of the self. In L. Berkowitz (Ed.), Advances in experimental social psychology, Vol. 21. Social psychological studies of the self: Perspectives and programs (pp. 261–302). Academic Press

10. Brown, B. (2012). Daring Greatly: How the Courage to Be Vulnerable Transforms the Way We Live, Love, Parent, and Lead. Gotham Books.

Brown, B. (2006). Shame resilience theory: A grounded theory study on women and shame. Families in Society: The Journal of Contemporary Social Services, 87(1), 43–52.

faithful, reach out, launch it, pitch it, say it. Say yes while your voice still shakes. You can even write a declaration or prayer that begins with: "Even when I don't feel ready, I will show up because..." Let your words ground you. Let your movement remind you that clarity is often waiting on the other side of obedience.

#MOVEANYWAY

You've made it to the end of a hard chapter, not just in this book, but maybe in your life too. And if nothing else, I hope you see this now: you were never behind, never too late, and never lacking. You were just buried under the weight of everyone else's noise and the belief that you had to do it their way.

Comparison, control, and the craving for certainty will keep showing up. But now you know how to recognize their disguises. Now you have tools to help you pause, pivot, and keep moving anyway. The path forward doesn't have to be perfectly paved; it just has to be yours. And the truth is, you're more ready than you think.

Before you turn the page, take a few moments for this final practice – the statement of truth and the journal prompt. Let it be your reset. Let it be your reclaiming.

Statement of truth:

I do not need certainty to take the next step. I do not need to match someone else's journey to make mine matter. I am no longer outsourcing my direction to comparison or control. I can trust the vision placed within me, enough to move, even when the path is unclear.

Journal Prompt

Where in your life have you let comparison rewrite the direction of your dream? What have you tried to control out of fear of uncertainty, and how has that shaped your decisions? What would it look like to move forward without knowing all the answers, but trusting that you are still enough?

Chapter 4

THEIR OPINIONS CAN'T BE THE REASON YOU STAY STUCK

*"When you shrink for others, don't be surprised
when they never ask you to grow."*

We've talked about how comparison can quietly take the wheel and steer your decisions before you even realize it. But there's another force, just as subtle, just as powerful, that can stall your momentum: the weight of other people's expectations, fears, and indecision.

Sometimes, what's holding you back isn't your own fear, but someone else's. And that's a harder truth to admit.

You may not call it that. You might say you're "being patient," "holding space," or "waiting until the timing feels right." But if you dig a little deeper, you'll find that you've tethered your next step to someone else's uncertainty. Their silence. Their indecision. Their unreadiness. And while it might look like love or loyalty on the surface, what it really becomes is a slow erosion of your own movement.

It doesn't always start as a conscious decision. Sometimes you delay your leap because you don't want to outpace your team, partner, friend group, or family. You wait, hoping they'll meet you at the edge, hoping they'll choose growth, hoping they'll see what you see and be brave with you. But what happens when they don't? What happens when their fear becomes your cage?

If you've ever paused a dream, delayed a decision, or dimmed your light because you didn't want to leave someone behind, you're not alone. I've done it too. It took me a long time to realize that waiting for someone else to feel ready was costing me the very momentum I needed to build my own life. And it's not always about romantic relationships either. This can appear in work partnerships, close friendships, creative collaborations, or even unspoken family dynamics. The outcome is the same: you end up waiting on a green light that's never coming.

This chapter is about naming that dynamic for what it is, and permitting you to choose forward motion even when someone else stays behind.

Not Everyone Will Go with You

Let me tell you a story. I'll use a metaphor to protect identities: a turtle and a ladybug.

Now, this wasn't just any turtle. This turtle was known for being bold in all the usual ways. Outgoing. Charming. A natural adventurer in his own right. He made people laugh, carried himself with confidence, and seemed to have life figured out. The kind of turtle others looked to for guidance and spark.

He lived in a wide-open meadow, a place he'd come to know well. It was beautiful. Predictable. Safe. He had built a good life there: steady, admired, and full of familiarity. But right beyond the edge of that meadow was a dense, mysterious forest. It was bigger, wilder, and full of potential he couldn't quite name, but deeply longed for.

He often talked about that forest, how it fascinated him. He imagined what life could be like beyond the tree line... but he never ventured in. He'd get close, maybe even poke his head past the last patch of grass, but each time, he'd retreat, telling himself that the meadow was good enough.

Enter the ladybug.

She was bright, intuitive, and bold in a different way. Where the turtle had charisma, she had clarity. She moved with ease between curiosity and courage, always searching for what came next. On her journey toward the forest, she spotted the turtle lingering at the edge, just close enough to see it, but not close enough to choose it. She paused, intrigued.

Their connection was immediate. The turtle opened up to her in ways he rarely had with anyone. He told her about the forest, how he longed to explore it, how he wasn't sure he could do it alone. And she believed him. She saw his heart. His hunger for more. And so, she offered: "We can go together."

He lit up. Said yes. Promised he was ready. But when she flew forward and looked back... he was still in the grass.

She returned. Encouraged him again. Reminded him of the dreams he'd named, the life he said he wanted. Again, he agreed. Again, he stayed behind.

Over time, she started to question herself. Wasn't she enough reason for him to try? Why wasn't their bond, their vision for what could be, strong enough to push him past his fear?

She began to shrink a little. To second-guess. Maybe she was asking for too much. Maybe she should wait longer, or quiet her own momentum so he didn't feel so pressured.

But something deeper rose up in her. A truth: you cannot want expansion for someone more than they want it for themselves. And if you stay too long at the edge of someone else's hesitation, you start convincing yourself that their decision is your limitation.

So, one last time, she returned. And said with love: "I care about you. I always will. But I can't stay stuck in the meadow just because you're not ready to enter the forest. I have to go, even if it means going alone."

And this time, she did.

That story might sound simple, but for me, it was personal. It mirrored a season in my own life when I realized I wasn't standing still out of fear... I was standing still out of loyalty to someone else's delay. I had the vision, and I was ready. But I kept circling a decision, waiting for someone else to meet me in the brave place.

And if you've ever felt that way too, know this: your future cannot wait indefinitely for someone else's permission. You were meant to grow beyond the meadow, even if they stay behind.

The Many Ways We Stay for Someone Else

Not everyone gets stuck for the same reason. Some of us overthink every possible outcome. Some of us wait for the perfect moment. And some of us get close, so close, and then stall out at the edge of something new. But here's what we don't always admit: sometimes, our stuckness isn't even about us. It's about the people we've tethered our progress to.

Take the overthinker. You might be like Overton, logical, careful, analytical. You map out the pros and cons of every possible step. But your internal alarms go off when someone you care about starts hesitating, doubting, or resisting change. You start overanalyzing for them, too. You try to factor in their emotions, readiness, and willingness to come with you, and suddenly, your bold move turns into a debate table in your head. You delay not because of your own uncertainty, but because you're weighing their indecision too heavily. You want to honor their process, but it's costing you your own momentum.

Or maybe you relate more to Patti, the perfectionist. You're committed, thoughtful, and intentional. You believe in doing things right, not just fast. So when someone you care about doesn't match your enthusiasm or commitment, you start to internalize it. If they don't want to go with me, maybe I'm being unreasonable. Maybe I'm too much. Maybe the timing really isn't right. You twist yourself into a version that feels more acceptable or accommodating, all while putting your own dreams on pause. You stay in the meadow, even though your heart is longing for the forest.

And then there's Alex, the almost-starter. You've gotten close so many times. You've planned the route, packed the bags, and even told a few people you were on your way. But every time you see someone you care about wavering, you convince yourself to delay, just a little bit longer. You say, They just need time. I'll wait. I'll hold off until they're ready so we can go together. And before you know it, months or years have passed, and you're still waiting. Not because you're afraid, but because you're loyal. Because you care. Because you didn't want to leave them behind.

These patterns don't make you weak. They make you human. But if we're not careful, our empathy becomes our excuse. Our love becomes our leash. And our potential stays parked in the meadow, waiting for someone else's permission to grow.

And it's not always about romantic or deeply personal ties. Sometimes, we stall because we've anchored ourselves to a mentor's approval, a leader's validation, or a peer's example. We hold off on launching the idea, switching paths, stepping forward because someone we look up to hasn't done it yet, or worse, doesn't believe we should. Their silence, hesitation, or disapproval can carry weight we were never meant to carry. But here's the truth: waiting for permission from someone who doesn't share your vision is one of the fastest ways to abandon your own.

Stuck by Association: How Other People's Hesitation Becomes Your Habit

Overton doesn't lack ideas; he lacks clarity because he's constantly scanning the room for consensus. Patti doesn't move because she's measuring her every step against how she'll be perceived. And Alex?

They get so close to a breakthrough, but abort the mission if the people they admire don't approve or understand. What all three of them are doing is externalizing their compass.

And science backs this up.

According to a study in *Psychological Bulletin*, individuals high in public self-consciousness (those deeply attuned to how others perceive them) are more likely to delay decisions, avoid risk, and conform to others' expectations—even at the cost of their own desires and goals[11]. In other words, the more you care about others' opinions, the more likely you are to stay stuck trying to be seen instead of moving.

This shows up in boardrooms and breakrooms alike. A 2022 survey by Asana found that 74% of employees hesitate to take initiative or share new ideas due to fear of judgment or lack of support from leaders[12]. That hesitation isn't laziness, it's social survival. Our brains are wired to prioritize belonging over boldness. Neuroscientist Matthew Lieberman's research at UCLA confirms that the same brain regions activated during physical pain are activated when we experience social rejection[13]. So it's no wonder we hesitate when moving forward risks losing connection, approval, or safety.

Even worse? When we're surrounded by indecisive or risk-averse people, we start to mirror their behavior unconsciously. This phenomenon, known as social modeling, is deeply embedded in human cognition. According to Bandura's Social Learning Theory, we often adopt behaviors based on what we observe in others, particularly those we admire or consider leaders[14]. So if a respected mentor doesn't leap, we might stay grounded too, even when everything in us is ready for takeoff.

Overton keeps polling others for reassurance, hoping someone will greenlight his decision. Patti holds back a proposal because her

11. Mor N, Winquist J. Self-focused attention and negative affect: a meta-analysis. Psychol Bull. 2002 Jul;128(4):638-62. doi: 10.1037/0033-2909.128.4.638. PMID: 12081086.
12. Asana. (2022). Anatomy of Work Global Index
13. Eisenberger NI, Lieberman MD, Williams KD. Does rejection hurt? An FMRI study of social exclusion. Science. 2003 Oct 10;302(5643):290-2. doi: 10.1126/science.1089134. PMID: 14551436
14. Bandura, A. (1977). Social Learning Theory. Englewood Cliffs, NJ: Prentice Hall.

team lead didn't offer upfront praise. Alex rewrites their business idea for the seventh time because their friend group didn't "get it." But what they're all really doing is outsourcing their momentum.

At some point, we must ask: Whose voice is in my head when I hesitate? And why does it get to take up that much space?

Detach. Decide. Do.

So, how do you actually move forward when someone else's opinion, silence, or hesitation is the very thing keeping you stuck?

You don't just wish your way out of it. You work your way out by learning to untangle their fear from your future. Whether you're circling a decision that affects your career, creative projects, or personal life, the key is learning to separate your internal resistance from your external reality. Let's break this down into three phases: Detach, Decide, Do.

Detach: Name Whose Fear You're Carrying

Psychologists call this emotional enmeshment, when your goals, decisions, and even your emotional responses become subconsciously tied to someone else's approval or behavior. According to research published in the Journal of Social and Personal Relationships, people who overidentify with others' expectations experience higher levels of anxiety and decision paralysis.

Start here:

- Write down the last 1-2 decisions you've stalled on. Ask yourself: Whose voice is in my head when I hesitate? Is it mine, or someone else's?
- Then, use the "Ownership Filter." For each decision, complete this sentence: "If I were the only one impacted, I would..." This helps surface where external opinions are creating internal blocks.

Overton, for example, might realize he's overanalyzing a business idea because his former boss once said entrepreneurship was too risky. Patti might delay launching her radio show because her partner doesn't understand her creative goals. And Alex? They might be waiting for validation from a mentor who always seems "too busy" to support them, forgetting that their growth isn't their responsibility.

Decide: Cut the Cord Without Cutting the Person

Detaching doesn't mean you stop caring. It means you stop deferring your progress to someone else's comfort level.

According to self-determination theory[15], autonomy, the ability to make choices that reflect your own values, is critical to sustained motivation. When you override your own instinct to avoid discomfort in a relationship, you end up weakening your sense of agency.

Try this:

♦ Visualize the "Life Delay Cost"

  ♦ Ask: If I wait six more months for this person to be on board… what opportunities do I miss? (Make the cost visible.)

♦ Use language that creates boundaries, not battles. For example:

  ♦ "I care about you deeply. But I've realized I've been putting parts of my life on hold out of fear that I'll lose your support. I'm ready to move forward anyway, not in spite of you, but because this matters to me."

This helps you draw a line without burning a bridge. And for those who aren't in direct conflict, like Patti's partner, who silently judged her ambition, you can still make a quiet internal decision: I'm not shrinking for their comfort anymore.

Do: Build Momentum With Micro-Boldness

This is where movement begins. And neuroscience tells us that even tiny acts of courage can rewire the brain's response to fear.

According to a 2021 study in *Biological Psychiatry*, activating the prefrontal cortex through intentional action helps regulate the amyg-

15. Deci, E. L., & Ryan, R. M. (2000). The "what" and "why" of goal pursuits: Human needs and the self-determination of behavior. Psychological Inquiry, 11(4), 227–268.

dala, which is responsible for our fear response[16]. Translation: Small, purposeful actions help calm the part of your brain that wants to keep you stuck.

Pick your micro-bold move: Send the email. Make the call. Say the thing. One bold action today builds the mental muscle to make bigger moves tomorrow. List one thing you can do that feels 10% bolder than yesterday. That's it. No need to leap, just stretch.

And finally, identify one "boldness witness." Tell one trusted person your next step, so you're not doing this alone. Research from the American Society of Training and Development shows that having accountability increases follow-through by up to 65%.[17]

Strategy Over Sympathy: Practical Moves That Put You Back in Motion

It's one thing to notice the influence of others; it's another to navigate it. These practical strategies are designed to help you recalibrate your choices, clarify your direction, and reclaim agency in the presence of relational pressure, social expectation, and comparison fatigue. Here are a few strategies to get you back in motion:

The 72-Hour Rule

When someone else's indecision causes your momentum to stall, create a pause window, no longer than 72 hours, to wait for clarity or confirmation. After that, you move forward, regardless of their timeline. Research suggests that prolonged decision paralysis under social pressure can increase anxiety and reduce long-term confidence in personal agency.

Feedback Filters

Before accepting someone's opinion, ask: Do they have the life or values I want? Are they responding from fear or faith?

---

16. Zhang, J., Liu, X., Liu, T., & Wang, Y. (2021). Prefrontal cortex activity mediates the regulation of fear via micro-action-based exposure. Biological Psychiatry, 89(12), 1112–1121.
17. Matthews, G. (2010). Accountability and follow-through: The power of commitment in goal achievement. American Society for Training and Development (ASTD) Research Review.

Use this to differentiate helpful advice from projection. Studies show that individuals often internalize the limiting beliefs of influential others, especially in close relational networks, which can compromise goal pursuit and risk-taking behavior.

Reverse Mentorship Reflection

If you're delaying a decision because a mentor or admired figure isn't moving or supporting you, ask: "What would I tell them if the roles were reversed?" Leadership psychology studies confirm that role reversal exercises boost confidence and diminish the internalized authority of perceived role models.

As a bonus practice, set a "Permission Statement" as your phone background. Examples include: I'm allowed to move without a map; Their doubt is not my direction; or I can be kind and still move on.

You can only sit at the edge of your own potential for so long before the ache to move becomes louder than the fear to stay. This chapter wasn't just about recognizing who or what's been holding you back; it was about reclaiming the power you gave away. Now, the question becomes: What do you want to do with it? The next step isn't about proving yourself to anyone else. It's about defining your direction, owning your identity, and choosing what kind of impact you're ready to make, with or without a cheer squad.

The waiting is over. Let's get intentional.

#MOVEANYWAY

You can only circle the edge of your own forest for so long before the call to move drowns out the comfort of staying. The turtle can choose the meadow. But you? You're the one with wings.

This chapter wasn't about villainizing the people you care about — it's about refusing to let their pace dictate your purpose. It's about recognizing the moment when loyalty becomes a leash, and deciding you won't keep yourself small to match someone else's fear.

You've been entrusted with a vision that is yours to carry. Whether others come along is their choice. Whether you move forward is yours. And the truth is, you don't need a unanimous vote to start. You need a single, decisive yes — your own.

The waiting is over. It's time to stop hovering at the edge and take your first step into the forest. Not to prove them wrong, not to leave them behind, but to live the life that keeps calling you forward.

The next step isn't about proving yourself to anyone else. It's about defining your direction, owning your identity, and choosing what kind of impact you're ready to make, with or without a cheer squad.

And if you need a reminder when the doubt creeps back in, let it be this: your life doesn't wait for someone else's green light.

Statement of truth:

I refuse to pause my purpose for people who aren't ready to grow with me.

Journal Prompt

Who have I been waiting on, and what is it costing me to keep shrinking while they stand still?

Chapter 5

YOUR BOLDPRINT: HOW TO BUILD A STRATEGY THAT FITS YOU

"The way you begin doesn't have to look like anyone else's blueprint. That's the beauty of building your own."

You've done the reflecting. You've named the fears. You've addressed the opinions of others. You've allowed my personal story and the stories of Overton, Patti, and Alex to help you better understand how overthinking, perfectionism, and almost-starts show up in your world. And now, it's time to trade the reflection loop for the clarity of action. Because here you are, still unsure of how to turn your ideas into something real. Not because you're unmotivated, but because you've never been given the space to build a plan that fits you.

Not the version of you that performs well on paper. The real you. The one who's juggling ambition and exhaustion, carrying unspoken dreams while secretly wondering if it's already too late. The one who overthinks every move, perfects every detail before acting, or hesitates so long that the moment passes entirely. If that's you, then you're not alone. You're ready for a shift!

This is the shift that changes everything.

But let's be clear: this chapter isn't about forcing yourself into some rigid, high-stakes hustle. It's not about pretending to be fearless, flawless, or fast. In this book, Boldness isn't defined by risk or volume—it's defined by alignment. It's about making moves that are rooted in your own voice, not someone else's expectations.

And that's where The BOLDprint Method comes in.

This is not a blueprint. Blueprints are rigid, technical, and built for duplication. They're designed to be followed by the letter, perfect lines, perfect angles, predictable outcomes. But you are not a copy-and-paste project. You are not a template.

You have been uniquely designed, with a set of God-given gifts, talents, ideas, and a calling that no one else can replicate. That uniqueness is not random, it's intentional. And with it comes responsibility. The impact you're meant to make isn't just about personal fulfillment; it's about collective transformation. When you move, others are freed to move too.

Your BOLDprint is the strategy, rhythm, and language that aligns with your divine wiring. It's your roadmap to move forward in the face of fear, not because you're certain, but because you're called.

And right now, our world is flooded with fear and doubt. People are overwhelmed, second-guessing, and settling. But imagine what could happen if more of us started moving from a place of truth instead of comparison. What if we stopped waiting to be chosen and started choosing to show up, with what we already have, right where we are?

That's what The BOLDprint Method offers: a personal plan for getting unstuck, moving forward, and fulfilling your purpose. Not someday, but now.

But how do you actually activate it?

That's where the B.O.L.D. framework comes in. It's not just a catchy acronym, it's a roadmap forged from research, real-life results, and the lessons I've learned from walking through doubt, detours, and divine nudges myself. I created a framework to help people like you recognize, unleash, and fully utilize their unique BOLDprint.

Each part of this framework speaks directly to what often holds us back: comparison, uncertainty, indecision, and fear. But when you move through it step by step, it helps you shift from stuck to strategic, and from overthinking to aligned action.

So, let's begin with the first, and one of the most important, moves you'll need to make: B – Block Out Comparison.

Chapter 6

YOU CAN'T WIN THEIR RACE

The "B" in the B.O.L.D. Framework – Block out comparison

Build What's Yours, Not What's Trending

You've made it this far in the book, which means you're doing more than thinking; you're preparing to build. To design a path that fits you, not one built from someone else's timeline, tools, or talents. But before we can put plans to paper, we have to address the invisible force that threatens to shape everything before you even begin.

That force is comparison.

As mentioned in Chapter 3, comparison is the single most common culprit of stuckness. It distorts your decisions before you take your first step. It tells you that someone already did it, already did it better, and already has more likes to prove it.

And yet, we rarely name it. We say we're "researching." We say we're "not ready yet." But what we're really doing is measuring the distance between someone else's success and our own starting point and then using that distance as proof that we're not enough. It doesn't start as self-doubt. It starts as admiration. Inspiration. Curiosity. But left unchecked, it becomes a self-made obstacle to your own bold moves.

You cannot build your BOLDprint while carrying the blueprint of someone else's life. That's why blocking out comparison is the first step in the method. Not because comparison is a flaw, but because it's a habit, and like any habit, it can be unlearned.

Quieting The Noise to Reclaim Your Voice

When you're finally ready to try something bold, something true to who you are, your brain immediately looks for what's familiar. This is especially true if you're entering a new space, making a career change, or finally starting the thing, you've been sitting on for months or even years. In uncertainty, your brain searches for examples, past models, or proven results.

And this is where things get tricky.

Because instead of looking inward at your own story, you start scanning outward. You look for people doing something similar. You measure their results. You analyze their style. You guess how long it took them to get there. And without realizing it, their roadmap becomes your ruler. You're no longer building your BOLDprint, you're building a weaker replica of someone else's work.

This is how:

- Overthinkers use comparison as permission to delay. They over-analyze others' moves until they've exhausted their own confidence.

- Perfectionists use comparison to upgrade the standard they've set for themselves, often making it so high it's impossible to reach.

- Almost-starters use comparison as a quiet way to self-disqualify. If someone else is doing it better, why even begin?

The problem isn't admiration, it's absorption. It's taking in so much of what others are doing that you lose sight of what's yours to do.

If comparison is the thief of joy, then clarity is the alarm system that helps you take it back. But clarity doesn't just arrive on its own; it's built, nurtured, and protected. That's what the research shows us: overcoming comparison isn't about ignoring others. It's about intentionally returning to yourself.

A study published in *The Journal of Positive Psychology* found that individuals who practice self-compassion are far less likely to fall into the trap of negative social comparison. Instead of spiraling into self-critique, they experience moments of "gentle accountability," a mindset that acknowledges where they are while still believing in where they're going. This is particularly powerful for overthinkers, who tend to inflate others' successes while shrinking their own. Cultivating self-compassion, especially through practices like affirmations or mindful breathing, helps reduce the shame-based thoughts that comparison often triggers.[18]

Speaker and educator Ben Nemtin shared how gratitude is an antidote to comparison in a TEDx talk. His method, called the "reverse gap," flips the script. Instead of obsessing over how far you are from where you want to be, you start by recognizing how far you've come. This technique doesn't just help perfectionists stop moving the goalpost; it allows them to see that progress already exists. When used regularly, this habit becomes a built-in checkpoint to pause, breathe, and reset the lens you're using to evaluate yourself.[19]

Finally, a meta-analysis in *Behavioral Sciences* explored the impact of creative expression on comparison stress. Researchers found that activities like journaling, sketching, and even simple voice note reflections allow individuals to re-anchor themselves in the present moment. These flow-state activities reduce the mental chatter of who's ahead or behind and bring attention back to the process rather than the outcome. For almost-starters, this kind of immersion in

18. Neff, K. D., & Germer, C. K. (2022). The Mindful Self-Compassion Workbook: A Proven Way to Accept Yourself, Build Inner Strength, and Thrive. The Guilford Press.
19. Nemtin, B. (2022). TEDx Talk: What Do You Want to Do Before You Die?

their own ideas can help build momentum before any external validation is needed. It's not about performance, it's about presence.[20]

What these studies show is that comparison doesn't disappear on its own. It's displaced by truth, gratitude, and flow. The more consistently you feed those three things, the less space there is for your confidence to be shaped by someone else's narrative.

Mirror Mirror On The Wall (Or Really Inside My Head)

You've just seen what the research says that comparison distorts truth, narrows your vision, and traps your potential in someone else's timeline. But theory only takes us so far. What happens when the algorithm feeds you someone else's highlight reel at your lowest moment? When your creative spark dims because you're convinced it's already been done better? When you're not just scrolling, but you're spiraling?

That's when the mirror gets loud. Not the actual mirror, but the mental one, the inner voice that starts with: "Why don't I look like that?" "Why am I not as far along?" "Why does it seem so easy for everyone else?" We've all had that moment, the one where you stop seeing your own potential and start seeing your reflection through the lens of lack. But behind every polished post you compare yourself to, there's a real human story... and you've got one, too.

Let me introduce you to someone who faced that spiral, and what it took to quiet the mirror and reclaim their lane. My former client, Malik, was a seasoned Chief People Officer with a track record that spoke for itself, transforming outdated workplace cultures, building inclusive leadership pipelines, and coaching senior executives through high-stakes change. But he started to unravel when his company elevated him to a more visible public-facing role, keynotes, panels, podcasts, and thought leadership.

---

20. Niles AN, Haltom KE, Mulvenna CM, Lieberman MD, Stanton AL. Randomized controlled trial of expressive writing for psychological and physical health: the moderating role of emotional expressivity. Anxiety Stress Coping. 2014 Jan;27(1):1-17. doi: 10.1080/10615806.2013.802308. Epub 2013 Jun 6. Erratum in: Anxiety Stress Coping. 2014 Jan;27(1):I. PMID: 23742666; PMCID: PMC3830620.

At first, he tried to play the game. He followed the "top voices" in leadership, workplace psychology, and DEI. He reshared popular posts. He even drafted a few carousels slides with sleek quotes and buzzwords. But nothing felt quite right.

By the time he and I met, Malik was stalled, not in his impact, but in his confidence to show up publicly without feeling like an imposter. He said, "It's like everyone else has this playbook, this perfect persona. And I'm showing up with Post-it Notes and real talk." Every time he logged onto LinkedIn, Malik's doubt deepened. His feed was a flood of viral thought threads, speaking reels, and "Top 40 Under 40" announcements. And while he genuinely celebrated others, he couldn't help but wonder: Where do I fit in this landscape of digital perfection?

What he didn't realize yet was that he was caught in a dangerous loop of performance fatigue, the mental and emotional exhaustion that sets in when you believe you must curate your worth before expressing it. It's the burnout of constant comparison. And as psychologist Tracy Dennis-Tiwary describes it, this is often fueled by ambient anxiety, that low-level hum of fear that you're not doing enough, even when you're doing everything you can.[14]

During one of our strategy sessions, I introduced him to a tool I call the "Legacy Log". It's not a resume. It's a receipt book for your real impact. I asked him to spend a weekend jotting down specific moments when his work made a difference—team culture shifts, individual breakthroughs, messages of appreciation, or ripple effects he helped create.

By Monday, he showed up differently.

He had written down stories of mentoring a junior HR associate who went on to lead her own team, of helping his CEO navigate a sensitive workforce reorganization, and of initiating a company-wide listening tour that became a model for other departments. The power of remembering his own gifts, his talents, his values, and his voice re-centered him.

And that week, Malik posted his first blog in over a year. It didn't have a fancy quote card or a polished hook. It had truth. It had perspective. And most importantly, it had him.

And it all started with stepping out of the comparison spiral and reclaiming the value of his real, lived impact.

Let's Build Your Legacy Log

Comparison tries to convince you that what you've done doesn't count. That you're not enough. That the way others show up is the only way to succeed. But the truth? You already hold the receipts. This practice is about reclaiming them, and moving forward from your lane, not someone else's feed. Here's how to begin:

Revisit Your Real Impact

Just like Malik, start by making a private list, not of accolades or titles, but moments of impact. Ask yourself: When did someone thank me for how I showed up? What ripple effects have I helped create that no one saw? What change have I sparked in quiet ways? Don't edit or shrink your responses. Write down the big and small wins that matter to you, not just what looks good on LinkedIn.

Re-anchor to Your 'Why'

Instead of obsessing over what's trending, ground yourself in what's true. Choose three core values that define how you want to lead, create, or show up. Not sure where to start? Think of the moments when you felt most yourself, most alive, and most honest. Your values often live there. Write them down. Post them where you can see them often. Use them as your decision filter moving forward.

Take Micro-Bold Actions This Week

Pick one way to show up in your own lane, without the pressure to perform. Maybe it's writing a post in your authentic voice. Maybe it's leading a team meeting in a way that reflects your values, not the script. Maybe it's texting a friend to remind them of their impact, because comparison doesn't win when we celebrate others from a place of wholeness. Whatever you choose, make it real and rooted in you.

You can use the Legacy Log template below as a way to start practicing logging your answers. Come back to this when you need support in blocking out comparison and staying in your own lane.

My Impact	My Why	My Micro-Bold Actions

What You Accomplished Still Counts

If you've worked through the last section, especially if you took the time to complete your Legacy Log, you've already done something powerful. You chose to look inward instead of outward. You interrupted the mental comparison loop and created space to see yourself again. That is no small thing. In fact, it's one of the hardest, boldest moves you can make in a world that constantly pressures you to measure your worth by someone else's ruler.

But now that you've cleared the noise, we have to ask: what will you fill that space with?

Because choosing your own lane is just the beginning, what sustains you in that lane is evidence. Real, lived proof that you have walked through hard things, made decisions under pressure, created beauty from messiness, and shown up when it would've been easier to hide. These aren't just accomplishments, they're anchor points. And remembering them doesn't just build confidence, it builds capacity.

The next part of this methodology is about gathering that evidence. I'm not just talking about awards or promotions, though those count too. Not the highlight-reel moments curated for social media, but the deeper wins, the personal breakthroughs, the quiet acts of courage, the decisions no one clapped for but that changed everything. The moments of grit, grace, clarity, and creativity that you've lived through, led through, and risen from.

You don't need to reinvent yourself. You need to remember yourself.

So in this next chapter, we'll unpack the "O" – by learning how to outline your past wins and successes. You'll see how those moments form the foundation of your BOLDprint, not because they were perfect, but because they were yours.

#MOVEANYWAY

Statement of truth:

I wasn't made to match; I was made to lead, in a way only I can. The moment I stop watching their race, I will finally find my own rhythm.

Journal Prompt

What stories, expectations, or comparisons have made you question your own path? Where can you reclaim your voice and start running your race at your own pace?

_____

_____

_____

_____

_____

Chapter 7

YOU KNOW MORE THAN YOU'RE LETTING ON

The "O" in the B.O.L.D. Framework –
Outline your past wins & successes

You've Been Bold Before, Let's Prove It

It's hard to believe in forward momentum when you've forgotten where you've already triumphed. That's why, once you block out comparison, the next bold move isn't to look ahead, it's to look back, not with regret or over-analysis, but with reverence. If comparison makes you forget who you are, reflection helps you remember what you've survived.

This step of the B.O.L.D. framework isn't just motivational, it's foundational. When you Outline Your Past Wins, you're not performing nostalgia. You're building your case. You're collecting the receipts of the moments where you chose courage, creativity, leadership, or persistence, even when no one saw it. For overthinkers, this short-circuits the analysis loop. For perfectionists, it reminds you that progress already happened without being flawless. For almost-starters, it shows that even micro-movements have always mattered.

And this is where faith meets strategy.

Legacy Stones of Remembrance

In the Bible, the book of Joshua highlights a key story about the Is-raelites. After the Israelites crossed the Jordan River, God gave them a command that was more than symbolic; it was deeply purpose-ful. He told them to gather twelve stones from the riverbed and set them up as a memorial, not just as a marker of their journey, but as a testimony for future generations. "When your children ask in time to come, 'What do these stones mean to you?' then you shall tell them…" (Joshua 4:6 - 7). These stones were physical proof of God's power, presence, and provision. They represented what was once impossible, the crossing of an overflowing river, made possible by divine intervention. God knew how easily we forget, especially when we're facing new obstacles. And He knew we'd need reminders not only for our own faith but to pass down the stories of break-through to those coming behind us.

Your past wins, those moments of movement, survival, courage, and healing, are your modern-day memorial stones. They may not sit in a riverbed but they hold just as much power. These moments are not accidental. They are evidence of God's hand in your life. Too often, we downplay them because they didn't make headlines or didn't happen on someone else's timeline. But Heaven noticed. And the ripple effect of your "yes" still matters.

Reflecting on your wins isn't prideful, it's purposeful. It's a spiri-tual act of gratitude and alignment. It says, "I remember what You brought me through, and I recognize that I didn't get here alone." And even more, it anchors you for what's ahead. Because if God was faithful before, He will be faithful again. And someone else, your children, team, and community, needs to see the evidence that bold moves are possible with faith.

So, how do you start building your personal memorial? The kind of remembrance that anchors you when doubt creeps in, and re-minds you, and others, what God has already brought you through?

Let's walk through the research, the story, and the strategies. Because those stones you've been carrying? They're not just weight, they're witness.

The Psychology of Remembering What You've Overcome

When you're stuck, your brain rarely offers you a highlight reel. Instead, it replays missteps, delays, and open loops. But there's a scientific reason that reflecting on past wins, especially small, personal ones, can reignite forward momentum.

According to research from psychologist Albert Bandura, developing self-efficacy (the belief in your own ability to succeed) is critical to overcoming obstacles and taking on new challenges. One of the strongest predictors of self-efficacy is recalling previous mastery experiences, moments when you've succeeded despite struggle or fear.[21] This is especially important for overthinkers, perfectionists, and almost-starters, who often downplay their past success instead of obsessing over future failure.

Additional research published in the *Journal of Personality and Social Psychology* shows that reflecting on meaningful personal achievements, especially when connected to core values, activates the brain's default mode network, the area linked to self-reflection and motivation.[22] In short: remembering what you've overcome doesn't just make you feel good—it makes your brain more likely to take bold action again.

So how do we use this research in real life?

Here's one practice: create a ritual of "reverse planning." Instead of starting your day by asking, What do I need to do?, start by asking, What have I already done that proves I can handle this? Before tackling a new project or stepping into a high-stakes moment, take five minutes to write down three personal wins, professional or otherwise, that highlight your courage, persistence, or creativity. This

21. Bandura, A. (1997). Self-efficacy: The exercise of control. W.H. Freeman.
22. Kang, Y., Gray, J. R., & Dovidio, J. F. (2014). The neural correlates of reflective self-awareness: A focus on the default mode network. Journal of Personality and Social Psychology, 106(3), 532–542.

is especially powerful for those with perfectionist tendencies who need tangible reminders that success is not always sleek or linear.

For almost-starters, a strategy called "identity reinforcement" can help shift your mindset. People are more likely to act when they identify as the kind of person who does X, rather than focusing on outcomes. So instead of saying, I want to get better at public speaking, say, "I've already shown I'm the kind of person who speaks up, even when it's hard." This subtle shift trains your mind to connect past wins with current identity, and future action.

And finally, for those battling comparison or scarcity, try building a confidence timeline. Choose a 5-year window and write down one win per year. It might be launching a project, navigating a difficult season, or simply showing up consistently when it wasn't easy. This timeline doesn't just reflect your strength; it reframes your progress. You'll begin to see that you've already done bold things before. The BOLDprint isn't foreign to you. It's already in your DNA.

More Than A Resume

Let me introduce you to another client – Diane. Diane was the quiet backbone of a high-performing nonprofit. As Director of Community Engagement, she had led more than a dozen successful programs, secured major grants, and mentored a generation of new staff. But something shifted after being passed over for a promotion she deeply wanted. Doubt crept in like a slow fog, and suddenly her accomplishments didn't feel like they mattered.

"I just don't think I stand out," she confessed during one of our strategy sessions. "I'm not loud. I'm not flashy. Maybe I've just been... average all along."

That's when I gave her a simple but powerful assignment: Grab a stack of sticky notes, and for the next week, every time she remembered a win, big or small, write it down and put it on a blank wall. The only rule? She couldn't write it as a task completed; she had to write what trait it revealed about her.

At first, the wall was sparse. A few notes here and there: "Helped calm a board member during a crisis – trait: patience." "Wrote and won the $80k grant – trait: strategy." "Spoke at the community rally – trait: courage." But something happened as she kept going. The wall began to fill. Notes multiplied, and so did her perspective. Once a space of silent defeat, her office became a visual tribute to who she was and what she'd already survived and accomplished.

One morning, she called and said, "I think I've been looking at my resume and forgetting my legacy." The wall had become a mirror, one that reflected her strength back to her in bold color.

Now it's your turn to build your wall of truth too!

A Wall of Wins

This exercise isn't about accolades, it's about identity. It's about reclaiming what you already carry, especially when self-doubt tries to erase the evidence. Creating a sticky note Wall of Wins allows your past wins to become visible proof that you've done hard things before and can do them again. And more importantly, it helps you name the internal traits that made those wins possible.

Here's how it works: Set aside a blank section of a wall, window, closet door, or any surface where you can place sticky notes. Over the course of one week, write down moments that reflect your growth, grit, or grace. Don't just list achievements, identify the internal quality you used to make them happen. "Managed a team through transition" becomes "resilience." "Pitched a bold idea even though I was nervous" becomes "courage." As the wall fills, patterns will begin to emerge. You'll see that your boldness has already been showing up in quiet ways. You just needed a place to see it clearly.

Revisit the wall often. Add to it. Stand in front of it when fear tries to shrink you. This isn't just a personal development exercise, it's a visual, daily practice of self-affirmation. And for the overthinkers, the perfectionists, and the almost-starters, it's a tangible reminder that you're not starting from zero. You're building from a place that's already strong.

Okay, so now the wall is built. The wins are real. You've already proven your strength; now it's time to put that strength in motion. Bold moves aren't just born from belief but sustained by what comes next. The B.O.L.D. framework doesn't stop with remembering who you are. It asks: what will you do with that truth?

#MOVEANYWAY

 **Statement of truth:**

My past wins aren't just memories, they're proof! I've done bold things before, and I'll do them again.

 Journal Prompt

What's a moment that you're proud of that you haven't given yourself enough credit for? What does it reveal about the strengths you tend to overlook?

_____

_____

_____

_____

_____

Chapter 8

TWO STEPS AHEAD BEATS STANDING STILL

The "L" in the B.O.L.D. Framework – List your next two steps

The Shift Starts Here

We often hear that every journey begins with a single step, but the truth is, one step can still leave you standing in place. That's why this part of the framework isn't just about taking a step. It's about taking at least two. Because one step is a choice. Two steps shift your posture, your mindset, and your position. They create a sense of traction, forward momentum that your brain can register as progress. And that progress builds trust, not just in the process, but in yourself.

The stall often happens for overthinkers in the swirl of options: Should you go left or right? Is now the right time? What if you regret it? The internal traffic jam builds until you can't tell action from anxiety. For perfectionists, movement gets delayed by the desire to polish every possible outcome. And for almost-starters, momentum breaks down not because they don't have vision, but because they've convinced themselves they need more–more time, more knowledge, more confirmation.

This part of the framework, the "L" – which stands for list your next two steps, slices through all of that. It doesn't require a ten-step plan or a vision board. It asks you to choose two clear, doable actions that move you out of neutral and into drive. Because while vision is powerful, it's the steps that turn vision into change.

In this section, we'll dig into research-backed tactics that activate forward motion, share a real-world story of what these steps look like in practice, and introduce a few strategies you can start using today.

Motion Over Perfection: The Science Behind Small Starts

Research in neuroscience tells us that taking a deliberate action triggers the brain's reward center, releasing dopamine, a chemical that reinforces motivation and signals that progress has been made. But the catch is, a single step often doesn't register as meaningful enough to anchor lasting change. It can feel accidental or easily dismissed, especially if self-doubt is loud. However, when you take two intentional actions in a row, the brain begins to recognize a pattern, and patterns are what give rise to sustained momentum.[23]

This concept is closely aligned with a refinement of "implementation intentions," which originally emphasized creating an if-then roadmap to reduce ambiguity and increase follow-through. While helpful, newer research suggests that building implementation momentum, where two or more small steps are linked together, creates a more sustainable behavioral shift. When you know what's coming after the first step, you're less likely to quit when resistance shows up.[24]

This is particularly powerful for overthinkers who often ruminate on the "perfect" next move, or for almost-starters who've taken action before but never gained traction. The two-step strategy al-

23. Murayama K, Kitagami S. Consolidation power of extrinsic rewards: reward cues enhance long-term memory for irrelevant past events. J Exp Psychol Gen. 2014 Feb;143(1):15-20. doi: 10.1037/a0031992. Epub 2013 Feb 18. PMID: 23421444

24. Gollwitzer, P. M., & Sheeran, P. (2006). Implementation intentions and goal achievement: A meta-analysis of effects and processes. In M. P. Zanna (Ed.), Advances in experimental social psychology, Vol. 38, pp. 69–119). Elsevier Academic Press.

leviates the pressure to have the full plan. It invites you to choose progress over perfection and teaches your nervous system that movement is safe, even if the outcome isn't yet certain.

Founder and researcher of the Behavior Design Lab at Stanford University, Dr. BJ Fogg's work on "tiny habits" backs this up. His research demonstrates that the most successful behavior changes don't start with giant life overhauls, but with low-effort, high-consistency actions that build identity over time.[25] For perfectionists, this is a lifeline: your next two steps don't have to be big. They just have to be yours. And they have to come one after the other, without waiting for applause or certainty.

Building on this, additional researchers found that "fresh start moments," like the start of a week, a birthday, or even the first day of a new month, can psychologically separate people from their past mistakes and increase motivation toward a goal.[26] But here's the twist: you don't have to wait for a Monday or a milestone. You can create your own fresh start simply by taking back-to-back action. By stringing two steps together, no matter how small, you generate your own momentum and turn the present moment into a turning point.

You don't need a 10-step plan when life feels heavy and clarity feels elusive. You need two steps that remind you: you can still move. And when you move, again, you change your direction, posture, and sense of what's possible.

Let me show you what that looks like in real life.

Stuck In Strategy Mode

I first met Jordan during my time as a healthcare consultant (we'll call the firm "The Farm"), and we stayed loosely connected over the years. He was recently promoted to COO at a mid-sized health tech company and had always prided himself on being a steady, thought-

---

25. Fogg, B. J. (2019). Tiny Habits: The Small Changes That Change Everything. Houghton Mifflin Harcourt.
26. Dai, H., Milkman, K. L., & Riis, J. (2014). The fresh start effect: Temporal landmarks motivate aspirational behavior. Management Science, 60(10), 2563–2582. https://doi.org/10.1287/mnsc.2014.1901

ful leader. But when we caught up on a call, the calm in his voice was gone.

The Board had delivered a hard directive: immediately cut operational costs by 30%. And the math didn't lie. That meant layoffs. Deep ones.

"I've run the numbers, looked at restructuring plans, even mapped out who we could let go," he said. "But I can't seem to pull the trigger. Every path feels like I'm destroying trust, morale, maybe even the future of the company culture we've built."

He wasn't lacking a plan. He was paralyzed by the weight of it. Like many high-level leaders, Jordan had all the spreadsheets and scenarios ready. Still, emotionally, he was stuck in strategy mode, hoping that another week, another model, another pivot might spare him from having to choose.

"What's something you can do this week that doesn't solve the whole thing but helps you lead with integrity?" I asked. He thought for a moment. "Honestly... I could meet with my leadership team. Not to drop the decision, but to talk. To process it together. To ask them what they need before this becomes real."

That was step one: gather the people who could help him carry the weight. Step two came right after: invite feedback and co-create a compassionate, transparent strategy. That pair of actions; conversation and collaboration, moved him out of isolation and into leadership. The steps were small. But they were bold, because they reestablished movement.

Instead of isolating himself in executive paralysis, Jordan invited his leaders into the process. Together, they built a plan that included voluntary departures, reassignments, and even retention bonuses for those most affected. Was it still hard? Absolutely. But it didn't shatter the culture. It reinforced it.

Sometimes we think one big move will change everything. But boldness isn't about leaping, it's about linking the right steps together. Jordan didn't solve it all at once. But he chose two meaningful steps, and that's what broke the silence, sparked motion, and restored trust.

The Momentum Map

After Jordan decided to lead with honesty and courage, he didn't try to build a full-scale change management plan overnight. What he needed, and what so many of us need when the pressure is high and the stakes are real, was a directional anchor. Something that helped him (and his team) make movement feel possible, without needing all the answers upfront. That's how he stumbled into what I now call the *Momentum Map*.

Here's how it works: Instead of trying to plot out your full master plan, you simply identify two distinct but connected actions that you can take next. One is a catalyst move, something that helps unlock internal clarity. The other is a connection move, something that brings others along with you or helps test your thinking in the real world. The point isn't to be perfect but to be purposeful. Every time you complete this two-step rhythm, your brain rewards the progress. It shortens the distance between idea and execution and builds a rhythm that adult learners especially thrive in: reflection followed by action.

When I introduced this to Jordan, he used it to shape how he showed up during a critical three-week stretch. His catalyst move was carving out time for a 45-minute "truth write," a private document where he dumped his fears, concerns, and vision onto the page. That inner clarity gave shape to his voice. His connection move came when he scheduled three one-on-one conversations with department leaders, not to roll out a plan, but to ask, "What do you need most in the next 10 days to steady your team?" That feedback sparked early action and built trust. It wasn't a grand reveal. It was a series of small, directional steps.

The Momentum Map isn't just for high-level executives; it works whether you're trying to launch a creative project, repair a relationship, or figure out your next career move. The key is honoring the cadence: an inward step that brings you closer to truth, followed by an outward step that brings you closer to traction. It's what separates good intentions from forward movement.

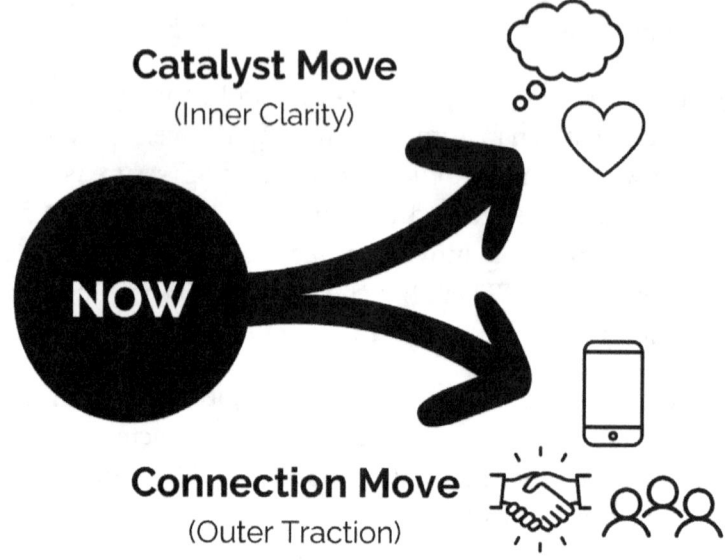

You've silenced the noise of comparison. You've gathered proof of your past wins. You've mapped out your next two steps. Now comes the most important shift of all: choosing to begin. Because all the clarity in the world means nothing if it's not met with action, that's what the final step in the B.O.L.D framework – "D" or Decide to Start Today, and we'll dive into it in the next chapter. Not waiting. Not rehearsing. But deciding to move forward, today, with what you already have. In the next chapter, let's talk about what that really takes.

#MOVEANYWAY

Statement of truth:

Momentum doesn't wait for certainty; it meets me in motion. I don't need the full plan to take my next two bold steps.

Journal Prompt

What are two next moves that you can take this week – even if they're small, messy, or imperfect – that will move me closer to what you want?

_____

_____

_____

_____

_____

Chapter 9

NO MORE WAITING ROOMS

The "D" in the B.O.L.D. Framework – Decide to start today

Ready or Not, It's Go Time

You've silenced the noise of comparison. You've gathered proof of your past wins. You've mapped out your next two steps. Now comes the most important shift of all: choosing to begin. Because all the clarity in the world means nothing if it's not met with action, that's what the final step in the B.O.L.D framework – "D" or Decide to Start Today. Not waiting. Not rehearsing. But deciding to move forward, today, with what you already have. Let's talk about what that really takes.

Every bold move eventually meets a fork in the road, the moment when ideas have been explored, fears have been named, and the next step is staring you down. That moment is now.

This is often the most uncomfortable part for overthinkers, perfectionists, and almost-starters. Because up until now, the work has mostly been internal: reflecting, remembering, imagining. But deciding? That means translating intention into action. It means leaving the safety of preparation and entering the uncertainty of motion.

But here's the truth: a decision is movement, even when it's small or not perfect. It's the difference between circling the runway and actually taking off between talking about the idea and becoming the person who does the thing.

And yet, so many people stall here. Not because they lack talent or insight, but because they've never been taught how to decide under uncertainty. They believe the lie that decisions should feel clean, confident, and final. But real decisions, the kind that shift your direction, often come with fear, ambiguity, and no guarantee of success. And still, they're worth making.

Overton second-guesses everything, replaying every "what if" like a loop. Patti keeps editing the perfect launch plan that no one has seen. And Alex waits for certainty to arrive, hoping clarity will feel like lightning when it comes. But here's the quiet truth each of them needs to hear: the fear won't always go away, but you can still choose anyway.

This section is about building the courage muscle required to move. Not someday. Today.

Let's explore what science and research say about how we actually make decisions, and how we can get better at it, even when fear is still in the room.

When Delay Becomes A Decision

Let's get one thing straight: not making a decision is a decision. You're choosing to stay still. And while it may feel like you're being careful or thoughtful, science says otherwise. Waiting too long can actually backfire.

In a study, researchers found that people presented with too many options tend to delay decisions, not because they're overwhelmed by complexity, but because they're afraid of making the wrong choice and regretting it later.[27] This "anticipated regret" often traps us in limbo. But here's the twist: those who made any choice, imperfect though it may be, reported greater satisfaction and progress than

27. Iyengar, S. S., & Lepper, M. R. (2000). When choice is demotivating: Can one desire too much of a good thing? Journal of Personality and Social Psychology, 79(6), 995–1006. https://doi.org/10.1037/0022-3514.79.6.995

those who stayed stuck. The takeaway? Waiting for the perfect decision delays the life you want.

And while we're here, let's bust another myth: that confidence comes before the decision. In fact, a study published in Nature Human Behaviour revealed that the act of committing to a decision increases confidence, even if you're still uncertain.[28] Participants who made firm choices showed improved clarity, cognitive ease, and long-term satisfaction compared to those who wavered or delayed. So no, you don't have to "feel ready" to move forward. You just have to move.

But what if fear is still hanging around? Research from the Yale Center for Emotional Intelligence offers a practical counter: naming the emotion out loud reduces its power.[29] Their findings show that "emotional labeling" calms the amygdala and activates the brain's prefrontal cortex, the part responsible for planning and decision-making. That means one of the simplest ways to push past fear is to actually say, "I'm scared," "I'm unsure," or "This makes me nervous." You take fear out of the shadows and put yourself back in the driver's seat.

In short: the science is clear. Bold decisions are not about certainty. They're about willingness. Willingness to risk being imperfect. Willingness to name the fear. Willingness to choose progress over paralysis. And each time you do, your decision-making muscles get stronger.

So now the question becomes: how do we use this? How do you go from knowing the research to acting on it? That's where we're headed next.

The Boldness Bet

There comes a point in every journey when hesitation costs more than the risk. You can overthink, rehearse, and run the options

28. Folke, T., Jacobsen, C., Fleming, S. M., & De Martino, B. (2020). Explicit representation of confidence informs future value-based decisions. Nature Human Behaviour, 4(3), 284–293
29. Lieberman, M. D., et al. (2007). Putting feelings into words: Affect labeling disrupts amygdala activity in response to affective stimuli. Psychological Science, 18(5), 421–428.

through your mind a hundred different ways. But eventually, you either stay in the cycle or you place your bet. And that's what this strategy is all about.

The Boldness Bet is a decision-making strategy rooted in movement psychology and micro-commitments. It helps you stop circling the idea and start moving toward it. Why? Because boldness isn't a personality trait, it's a wager. A bet you make on your own potential, even without perfect odds. And when you're stuck in delay or indecision, the most courageous thing you can do is make a move that says: I trust myself enough to go now. There are three steps:

1. The Decision at Stake – You name the thing you've been avoiding. Not vaguely, but clearly: the book idea you keep shelving, the career conversation you've been dodging, the health reset you keep saying you'll start Monday. You articulate the decision in real terms, because clarity is half the battle.

2. The Boldness Bet – Here's where it gets different. Instead of listing pros and cons (which often leads to more stalling), you name your bold hypothesis, what you believe could happen if you moved forward with courage. This bet is personal. It's your inner knowing, your gut instinct, your best-case vision. You also name the bet you're placing on yourself. What internal strength are you counting on, resilience, creativity, adaptability, intuition?

3. The Proof Point – Now, you pick two immediate, concrete actions you will take in the next 24 hours to back up that bet. Not something performative. Something that activates movement. Maybe you schedule the meeting. Launch the landing page. Make the phone call. These steps prove to your brain and spirit that you meant what you wrote.

By completing this strategy, you shift from "I want to" to "I'm already becoming." For overthinkers, it reduces the noise by forcing a singular focus. For perfectionists, it breaks the paralysis of needing every step to be flawless. For almost-starters, it marks the moment the fantasy becomes movement. The Boldness Bet interrupts the cycle of stalling by creating a moment of personal accountability that feels both empowering and real.

This isn't about betting recklessly, it's about betting intentionally, not with blind hope, but with bold trust. If you're going to bet on anyone, let it be the version of you who is brave enough to start today, even without all the answers.

THE BOLDNESS BET

I'm betting on...

_____

_____

_____

Because I know I already have...

_____

_____

_____

Here's how i'll start today...

_____

_____

_____

Proof point check-in date:

#MOVEANYWAY

Your path forward doesn't have to mirror anyone else's, and it shouldn't. You've just walked through a framework that wasn't built to impress the crowd but to empower YOU instead. The B.O.L.D. framework isn't about chasing more; it's about choosing well. It's about clarity over chaos, progress over perfection, and small moves that carry big meaning. Whether you're battling comparison, stuck in the cycle of overthinking, waiting for flawless timing, or wrestling with doubt, your BOLDprint gives you the strategy to move anyway. Not blindly. Not hastily. But with intention, courage, and self-trust. Now you know what to do and how to do it. The only thing left? Decide to start.

Statement of truth:

I don't need every answer to begin. Today, I'm choosing to simply start, because being stuck is no longer an option.

Journal Prompt

What bold decision have you been delaying, and what would it look like to start today, even if all you have is belief?

_____

_____

_____

_____

Chapter 10

KEEP THAT SAME ENERGY

How to Sustain Moving Forward
Without Burning Out

"Making a move is bold. But learning how to keep moving, that's what makes it lasting."

You've done something many people never get to: you moved. You pushed past the hesitation, the overthinking, the impossible standards, and the fear of a false start, and you moved anyway. That alone is worth celebrating. But what no one tells you is this: movement is one thing. Maintenance is another beast entirely.

Because boldness isn't a one-time act, it's a rhythm. It's a daily decision to keep showing up, even when the initial rush fades and the applause dies down. Anyone can sprint for a moment. But what about sustaining the stride when resistance kicks in, internally and externally? What about when life throws a curveball, when momentum gets interrupted, or when you start questioning whether it was all just a fluke?

This chapter is about that moment. The one where you're tempted to slip back into familiar patterns, not because you don't want change, but because consistency takes a different kind of courage.

And when you've built something meaningful, the stakes feel higher. You don't just want to move; you want it to last. You want your progress to hold. You want to stop starting over.

That's the hard truth about growth: It's not a highlight reel; it's a habit. The daily grind of holding on to what you've learned, applying it when no one's watching, and choosing not to sabotage the progress just because discomfort showed up at the door. This chapter isn't about hype. It's about habits. It's about the behind-the-scenes work required to make boldness sustainable, not performative.

And let's be real: this is where a lot of people tap out. They build the vision board, fill the journal with goals, maybe even take a leap... and then life starts life-ing. The urgency fades. Doubt creeps in. Old routines come knocking. The same thoughts that had you stuck before start whispering again, but softer this time, pretending to be logic or safety.

So, if you've ever wondered how to maintain bold action without burning out, keep going when the shine wears off, or stay steady even when no one's watching, this is for you.

Let's talk about how to keep that same energy... and why it matters more than ever.

Same You, New Moves: How Growth Evolves with You

It's one thing to read about growth, it's another to live it. And as you've probably discovered by now, the barriers you face don't disappear just because you made progress. They evolve. The fears resurface with new faces. The pressure shifts form. But the same patterns still try to creep in, just dressed in more convincing disguises.

So how do you keep moving forward without slipping back?

Let's revisit Overton, Patti, and Alex – our overthinker, perfectionist, and almost-starter. You've met them in earlier chapters, and maybe you saw your own reflection in their habits, fears, or patterns at some point. But here's the thing: each of them made a move. They took the leap. They embraced the uncomfortable. And now they're all facing a new challenge: how to keep going.

This is the moment where so many burn out. Or fizzle out. Or stall. But it doesn't have to be that way. Because whether you're wired to overanalyze every decision like Overton, polish every plan to death like Patti, or hesitate until the moment passes like Alex, the real opportunity now is to learn what sustainable boldness looks like for *you.*

Because moving once is brave, but learning how to keep that same energy, that's transformation.

Breaking the Loop: Overton's Shift Toward Intentional Action

Overton used to live in the loop, the mental merry-go-round where every decision felt like a trap and every option was overanalyzed until momentum died on the vine. He had brilliant ideas, sharp instincts, and a heart that wanted to do good in the world. But he also had a mind that whispered, "What if you get it wrong?" louder than it ever affirmed, "You're ready." He didn't lack ambition; he lacked a starting point that felt safe enough to trust.

Now? Overton still hears the whispers of doubt, but he doesn't entertain them like houseguests. Instead of replaying scenarios in his head, he takes one clear action. Then another. He's traded perfection for consistency and swapped planning paralysis for something more powerful: micro-bold momentum. He doesn't need the entire blueprint to be mapped out. He just needs his next two steps, and the belief that he can handle what comes after that.

He's built practices that keep him grounded: quick clarity sessions where he sets a timer and forces himself to name a next step, voice memos to himself when his insight is sharp but fleeting, and a running list of proof points, not just to boost his confidence, but to serve as undeniable evidence when his inner critic gets loud. When the fog of uncertainty creeps in, he doesn't try to control every outcome anymore. He anchors into the pattern he's seen – when he moves, clarity follows. His rhythm isn't frantic, it's intentional. And his version of boldness isn't about dramatic risks, but daily resolve. The kind that shows up even when no one is watching.

To all the Overtons reading this, sustaining your growth requires discipline, not just desire. Your mind may always offer ten reasons to pause, but your legacy will be built by the one reason you chose to move anyway. Create rituals reinforcing progress: document your wins, speak your goals out loud, and set deadlines you honor even when motivation fades. Don't wait for perfect conditions; they rarely come. Build a system that protects your momentum, especially on days when doubt feels louder than truth. You don't need to eliminate your overthinking; you need to outpace it.

Done > Perfect: Patti Redefines Success

Patti used to believe that everything had to be flawless before it could be seen. Her drafts were endless, her ideas hidden behind "almost ready," and her calendar packed with other people's priorities while her dreams sat quietly in the margins. But something shifted. She stopped waiting for the perfect time and started choosing better timing that aligned with her energy, calling, and capacity. Now, her work isn't perfect; it's impactful. And that's the point.

She's created boundaries with grace and systems that protect her creative flow. She's learned to deliver powerful work in phases, allowing room for feedback without tying her worth to the response. She's traded comparison spreadsheets and polished presentations for post-it notes of progress and gut-checked gut instincts. She doesn't drown in metrics anymore; she measures movement. The Patti of today knows that excellence isn't erased by imperfection, and she reminds herself often: done is divine.

For perfectionists like Patti, sustaining momentum looks like building self-compassion into the process. It means pausing to celebrate micro-wins, honoring when rest is needed, and resisting the urge to over-edit progress into paralysis. Sustainability doesn't come from doing it all; it comes from doing what matters most, consistently. Patti's growth is no longer measured in accolades or applause, but in alignment and action. And similar to her, you may still feel the pull to perfect, but don't let it steer you. Move anyway!

Start Small, Stay Ready: Alex's New Rhythm

Alex used to wait for the perfect moment, that magical, mythical time when clarity, confidence, and calm would all appear simultaneously. They had no shortage of passion or ideas, but their actions always arrived late... if they arrived at all. Opportunities passed them by, not because they didn't care, but because they kept convincing themselves that they weren't quite ready. But now? They've stopped waiting for the green light and started walking forward, even if the path is still being built as they move.

Alex doesn't confuse discomfort with danger anymore. They've learned how to quiet the mental checklist that says everything must be in place before a move can be made. Instead of asking, "Is this the right time?" they now ask, "Is this aligned with what I believe and where I'm headed?" That one shift changed everything. Today, they speak up in rooms they used to shrink in. They take the first step and let momentum meet them there. And when the old fear creeps in, they return to what they know now: movement builds confidence, not the other way around.

For the almost-starters like Alex, sustaining this shift means embracing small beginnings without shame. It means noticing when the instinct to pause is rooted in fear, not strategy. It means having a vision but being flexible with the path that leads there. Progress isn't linear, and perfection isn't required. What matters most is that you keep choosing to begin, again and again, even if it's messy or imperfect. Alex is no longer waiting for permission (and neither should you). Instead, keep showing up, trusting that the act of moving is what makes you ready.

When the Fire Fades: What It Takes to Keep Going When the Spark Doesn't

You've seen the shift. Overton rewired his decision-making patterns. Patti stopped hiding behind polish, and Alex gave themself permission to begin. These aren't just personality pivots; they're energetic recalibrations. But sustaining that energy is a different kind of challenge altogether.

Let's be honest: boldness is thrilling at first. The adrenaline of a new mindset, the validation of initial wins, and the clarity of a fresh strategy all feel like momentum until life gets loud again. Until fear disguises itself as logic. Until the spark that once fueled your forward motion starts flickering. Many face the reality after the breakthrough moment: fizzling out, not because they're weak, but because they didn't know that sustaining boldness requires more than the bold moment itself.

Research shows that the initial energy of a behavior change doesn't always guarantee sustainability. According to Dr. Katy Milkman at the University of Pennsylvania, we often experience a surge in motivation around what she terms "fresh start moments," beginnings like a new year, birthday, or new season. Still, that motivation tends to fade when progress slows or obstacles arise.[30] We love the idea of transformation more than the maintenance it requires. That's where burnout slips in quietly.

And burnout doesn't just affect your energy; it clouds your decision-making and shrinks your confidence. In fact, a study published in *World Psychiatry* found that burnout can lead to feelings of inefficacy and emotional exhaustion that closely mirror depression.[31] So when that energy dips, it's not just a productivity problem, it's a whole-self disruption. The thing you were once excited about now feels like a burden. That's why sustaining boldness isn't about pushing harder but adjusting smarter.

Resistance also changes forms. Sometimes it's internal, the self-doubt that whispers "you're falling behind" or "maybe this was a fluke." Other times it's external, like well-meaning friends or colleagues questioning your path because it makes them uncomfortable. In *The War of Art*, Dr. Steven Pressfield refers to this phenomenon as "Resistance

30. Milkman, K. L., Dai, H., & Riis, J. (2014). The Fresh Start Effect: Temporal Landmarks Motivate Aspirational Behavior. Management Science, 60(10), 2563–2582.

31. Maslach, C., & Leiter, M. P. (2016). Understanding the burnout experience: recent research and its implications for psychiatry. World Psychiatry, 15(2), 103–111.

with a capital R," a shape-shifting force that grows stronger the closer you get to your purpose. You're not imagining it. The friction is real.[32]

And for those who are used to high output, perfectionism, or people-pleasing, the trap is often overperformance. You finally make a bold move, and then you try to prove it was worth it by pushing yourself to exhaustion. That's not growth, that's self-sabotage dressed as achievement. Researchers Maslach and Leiter suggest that preventing burnout requires "sustainable engagement," where effort is balanced with rest, reflection, and realistic goals.[33] Not just because it feels good, but because it works long-term.

Here's why this matters for you: Your BOLDprint isn't just a plan to get moving, it's your personal (and unique) roadmap to help you keep moving, especially when things get hard, dull, or unpredictable. Because let's be honest: the glow of a new idea fades fast when routines kick in, results feel slow, and the people around you don't understand your shift. That's when you need something sturdier than hype. You need rhythm. You need reinforcement. That's what your BOLDprint offers, not just a jumpstart, but a system rooted in your values, strengths, and vision. Without that structure, you're left trying to power progress through willpower alone, and neuroscience confirms that willpower is a limited, depletable resource.[34]

So now what? You build safeguards around your energy. You create rhythms, not just goals. You normalize seasons of lower capacity without letting them erase your progress. You start asking better questions like: What helps me refill? What warning signs tell me I'm approaching burnout? Who are my accountability anchors? What needs to shift when resistance shows up again? Because it will. Resistance doesn't mean you've failed, it means you're still moving. And now, you have the tools to meet it, not with panic or perfectionism,

32. Pressfield, S. (2002). The War of Art: Break Through the Blocks and Win Your Inner Creative Battles. Black Irish Entertainment LLC.
33. Maslach, C., & Leiter, M. P. (1997). The Truth About Burnout: How Organizations Cause Personal Stress and What to Do About It. Jossey-Bass.
34. Baumeister, R. F., Bratslavsky, E., Muraven, M., & Tice, D. M. (1998). Ego depletion: Is the active self a limited resource? Journal of Personality and Social Psychology, 74(5), 1252–1265. https://doi. org/10.1037/0022-3514.74.5.1252

but with grounded, confident action. That's what sustainable bold-ness looks like.

This Is the Moment: Don't You Dare Stop Now

Let me be real with you: I don't write these words from a place of arrival; I write them from the middle. I'm walking through my own bold season right now. There are moments when resistance whis-pers, the "what ifs" get loud, and fear tries to knock on the door dressed up as logic or timing or being "responsible." But I move any-way. Not because it's easy. Not because I've mastered it. But because I've tasted what it's like to stay stuck, and I refuse to go back.

That's what I want for you.

This book, this whole journey, has never been about pushing you to do more. It's about inviting you to be more of who you already are. We've named the fears. We've deconstructed the lies. We've charted the course. And now you're holding the keys. You don't need more credentials or clarity or permission. You need one thing: a decision to keep moving. Because the cost of standing still is far greater than the risk of moving forward.

Listen, the world doesn't need a quieter version of you. It needs your full, unfiltered presence. Your voice. Your gifts. Your legacy. Ev-ery delay, detour, and loop of overthinking is stealing time and im-pact, not just from you, but from those waiting on what only you can offer. That idea? That change you want to see? That vision that keeps tugging at you? It's not random, it's assigned. And it won't come to life unless you choose to move.

So here it is – your invitation to stop romanticizing the plan and start honoring the process. To stop waiting for the fear to disappear and walk through it anyway. Progress is messy. Impact is inconve-nient. And change doesn't come from confidence; it comes from commitment.

You've got what you need. You've had it all along. I've just been here to push you forward, similar to how someone ('preciate ya Holy Spirit!) did the same thing for me.

Now... keep that same energy—and move anyway.

 **Final Statement of Truth:**

I will keep moving even when the spark fades or the fear returns. My momentum is mine to protect, and my purpose is too important to pause.

Repeat this statement each day for the next 7 days. Set a routine and commit to saying and believing this truth.

 Final Journal Prompt

What is one bold move you've been avoiding, but now feel called to make? What would it look like to move forward with what you have, from where you are, right now?

_____

_____

_____

_____

_____

REFERENCES

1. "Frick A, Björkstrand J, Lubberink M, Eriksson A, Fredrikson M, Åhs F. Dopamine and fear memory formation in the human amygdala. Mol Psychiatry. 2022 Mar;27(3):1704-1711. doi: 10.1038/s41380-021-01400-x. Epub 2021 Dec 3. PMID: 34862441; PMCID: PMC9095491" on page 14

2. "Gollwitzer, Peter. (1999). Implementation Intentions: Strong Effects of Simple Plans. American Psychologist. 54. 493-503. 10.1037/0003-066X.54.7.493" on page 32

3. "Barry Schwartz, "The Paradox of Choice," TED Talk, 2005." on page 33

4. "Fuschia M. Sirois and Timothy A. Pychyl, "Procrastination and the Priority of Short-Term Mood Regulation: Consequences for Future Self," Social and Personality Psychology Compass, vol. 7, no. 2 (2013): 115–127." on page 33

5. "Whelan, Eoin and Islam, Najmul and Brooks, Stoney, The Effects of Social Media Overload on Academic Performance (December 4, 2019)" on page 48
"Vogel, Erin & Rose, Jason & Roberts, Lindsay & Eckles, Katheryn. (2014). Social Comparison, Social Media, and Self-Esteem. Psychology of Popular Media Culture. 3. 206-222. 10.1037/ppm0000047" on page 48

6. "Shah, A. K., Mullainathan, S., & Shafir, E. (2012). Some consequences of having too little. Science, 338(6107), 682–685. https://doi.org/10.1126/science.1222426" on page 49

7. "Brown, B. (2012). Daring Greatly: How the Courage to Be Vulnerable Transforms the Way We Live, Love, Parent, and Lead. Gotham Books." on page 50
"Brown, B. (2010). The Gifts of Imperfection. Hazelden Publishing." on page 50

REFERENCES

8. "Wang W, Wang M, Hu Q, Wang P, Lei L, Jiang S. Upward social comparison on mobile social media and depression: The mediating role of envy and the moderating role of marital quality. J Affect Disord. 2020 Jun 1;270:143-149. doi: 10.1016/j.jad.2020.03.173. Epub 2020 Apr 5. PMID: 32339106." on page 52
   "Vogel, Erin & Rose, Jason & Roberts, Lindsay & Eckles, Katheryn. (2014). Social Comparison, Social Media, and Self-Esteem. Psychology of Popular Media Culture. 3. 206-222. 10.1037/ppm0000047" on page 52

9. "Oyserman, D., Bybee, D., & Terry, K. (2006). Possible selves and academic outcomes: How and when possible selves impel action. Journal of Personality and Social Psychology, 91(1), 188–204. https://doi.org/10.1037/0022-3514.91.1.188" on page 53
   "Steele, C. M. (1988). The psychology of self-affirmation: Sustaining the integrity of the self. In L. Berkowitz (Ed.), Advances in experimental social psychology, Vol. 21. Social psychological studies of the self: Perspectives and programs (pp. 261–302). Academic Press" on page 53

10. "Brown, B. (2012). Daring Greatly: How the Courage to Be Vulnerable Transforms the Way We Live, Love, Parent, and Lead. Gotham Books." on page 53
    "Brown, B. (2006). Shame resilience theory: A grounded theory study on women and shame. Families in Society: The Journal of Contemporary Social Services, 87(1), 43–52." on page 53

11. "Mor N, Winquist J. Self-focused attention and negative affect: a meta-analysis. Psychol Bull. 2002 Jul;128(4):638-62. doi: 10.1037/0033-2909.128.4.638. PMID: 12081086." on page 62

REFERENCES

12. "Asana. (2022). Anatomy of Work Global Index" on page 62

13. "Eisenberger NI, Lieberman MD, Williams KD. Does rejection hurt? An FMRI study of social exclusion. Science. 2003 Oct 10;302(5643):290-2. doi: 10.1126/science.1089134. PMID: 14551436" on page 62

14. "Bandura, A. (1977). Social Learning Theory. Englewood Cliffs, NJ: Prentice Hall." on page 62

15. "Deci, E. L., & Ryan, R. M. (2000). The "what" and "why" of goal pursuits: Human needs and the self-determination of behavior. Psychological Inquiry, 11(4), 227–268." on page 64

16. "Zhang, J., Liu, X., Liu, T., & Wang, Y. (2021). Prefrontal cortex activity mediates the regulation of fear via micro-action-based exposure. Biological Psychiatry, 89(12), 1112–1121." on page 65

17. "Matthews, G. (2010). Accountability and follow-through: The power of commitment in goal achievement. American Society for Training and Development (ASTD) Research Review." on page 65

18. "Neff, K. D., & Germer, C. K. (2022). The Mindful Self-Compassion Workbook: A Proven Way to Accept Yourself, Build Inner Strength, and Thrive. The Guilford Press." on page 75

19. "Nemtin, B. (2022). TEDx Talk: What Do You Want to Do Before You Die?" on page 75

REFERENCES

20. "Niles AN, Haltom KE, Mulvenna CM, Lieberman MD, Stanton AL. Randomized controlled trial of expressive writing for psychological and physical health: the moderating role of emotional expressivity. Anxiety Stress Coping. 2014 Jan;27(1):1-17. doi: 10.1080/10615806.2013.802308. Epub 2013 Jun 6. Erratum in: Anxiety Stress Coping. 2014 Jan;27(1):I. PMID: 23742666; PMCID: PMC3830620." on page 76

21. "Bandura, A. (1997). Self-efficacy: The exercise of control. W.H. Freeman." on page 85

22. "Kang, Y., Gray, J. R., & Dovidio, J. F. (2014). The neural correlates of reflective self-awareness: A focus on the default mode network. Journal of Personality and Social Psychology, 106(3), 532–542." on page 85

23. "Murayama K, Kitagami S. Consolidation power of extrinsic rewards: reward cues enhance long-term memory for irrelevant past events. J Exp Psychol Gen. 2014 Feb;143(1):15-20. doi: 10.1037/a0031992. Epub 2013 Feb 18. PMID: 23421444" on page 92

24. "Gollwitzer, P. M., & Sheeran, P. (2006). Implementation intentions and goal achievement: A meta-analysis of effects and processes. In M. P. Zanna (Ed.), Advances in experimental social psychology, Vol. 38, pp. 69–119). Elsevier Academic Press." on page 92

25. "Fogg, B. J. (2019). Tiny Habits: The Small Changes That Change Everything. Houghton Mifflin Harcourt." on page 93

26. "Dai, H., Milkman, K. L., & Riis, J. (2014). The fresh start effect: Temporal landmarks motivate aspirational behavior. Management Science, 60(10), 2563–2582. https://doi.org/10.1287/mnsc.2014.1901" on page 93

REFERENCES

27. "Iyengar, S. S., & Lepper, M. R. (2000). When choice is demotivating: Can one desire too much of a good thing? Journal of Personality and Social Psychology, 79(6), 995–1006. https://doi.org/10.1037/0022-3514.79.6.995" on page 100

28. "Folke, T., Jacobsen, C., Fleming, S. M., & De Martino, B. (2020). Explicit representation of confidence informs future value-based decisions. Nature Human Behaviour, 4(3), 284–293." on page 101

29. "Lieberman, M. D., et al. (2007). Putting feelings into words: Affect labeling disrupts amygdala activity in response to affective stimuli. Psychological Science, 18(5), 421–428." on page 101

30. "Milkman, K. L., Dai, H., & Riis, J. (2014). The Fresh Start Effect: Temporal Landmarks Motivate Aspirational Behavior. Management Science, 60(10), 2563–2582." on page 112

31. "Maslach, C., & Leiter, M. P. (2016). Understanding the burnout experience: recent research and its implications for psychiatry. World Psychiatry, 15(2), 103–111." on page 112

32. "Pressfield, S. (2002). The War of Art: Break Through the Blocks and Win Your Inner Creative Battles. Black Irish Entertainment LLC." on page 113

33. "Maslach, C., & Leiter, M. P. (1997). The Truth About Burnout: How Organizations Cause Personal Stress and What to Do About It. Jossey-Bass." on page 113

34. "Baumeister, R. F., Bratslavsky, E., Muraven, M., & Tice, D. M. (1998). Ego depletion: Is the active self a limited resource? Journal of Personality and Social Psychology, 74(5), 1252–1265. https://doi.org/10.1037/0022-3514.74.5.1252" on page 113

ABOUT THE AUTHOR

Krista D. Stepney is a leadership and business strategist, keynote speaker, and transformation advisor who helps leaders and everyday changemakers turn hesitation into momentum. With over 15 years of experience in operations, organizational leadership, and culture transformation, Krista blends research, faith, and lived experience to help others build a purposeful life and legacy.

As the creator of The BOLDprint Method and the W.A.N.D. methodology, she has coached executives, entrepreneurs, and everyday dreamers on overcoming fear, resisting comparison, and designing a personalized roadmap forward, even when the next step feels unclear.

Her mission is simple: to help people get unstuck and move anyway, especially when it feels like the hardest thing to do.

ACKNOWLEDGEMENTS

This book was born in the tension between fear and faith. This book could not have come to life without the people who reminded me, through their words, presence, and belief, that movement matters, even when it's messy.

Thank you to every client, overthinker, perfectionist, and almost-starter who trusted me with your stories, struggles, and stuck places. Your honesty lit the path and shaped every sentence.

To my personal Lord & Savior, Jesus Christ, thank you for your divine nudge that continues to propel me forward, even when I want to shrink back; I'm forever grateful for your unconditional love. This was more than a writing journey; it was a spiritual one. I now understand that boldness doesn't start with the crowd; it starts with a whisper.

To my core family trio – Chulo, Mommie, and Ginny: your unwavering belief in me, even when I questioned myself, has been my steady ground. Thank you for holding space, cheering loudly, and reminding me that rest is not the opposite of progress. Thank you for always asking me, "Who are you?" That question, which started as a joke, has been a constant reminder to be ready to answer that question boldly, even when the answer scares me.

To my K Krew leadership team (Kels, Janelle, and Allegra Claire), my editing guru (thank you for pulling out your editing pen for me, Mrs. Rita), my ultimate researcher and the baddest PhD that I know (I see you Dr. Portia aka Hazel), and my confidants (thank you to my HIVE, my 16 closest ladies, and my Dallas, TX core girls) who reminded me to move anyway even on the hard days – this work bears your fingerprints. I'm grateful beyond measure for your encouragement and your wisdom.

To the turtle...may you find this book a reminder that you already have everything you need within you to be bold and to get out of your own way. Go be great!

And finally, to you, the reader. You've made it to the final page, and that means something. I appreciate you allowing me into your space of vulnerability. I pray that what you've read lingers longer than motivation and becomes movement.

Now go. Your boldest chapter is waiting.

www.ingramcontent.com/pod-product-compliance
Lightning Source LLC
Chambersburg PA
CBHW071521120626
46550CB00006B/2308